ID625977

a nest egg for your family

Saving and Investing for Your Children

How to build a nest egg for your family

Moira O'Neill

A & C Black • London

First published in the United Kingdom in 2009 by

A & C Black Publishers Ltd
36 Soho Square, London W1D 3QY
www.acblack.com

Copyright © Moira O'Neill, 2009

The Guardian is a registered trademark of the Guardian Media Group plc.
Guardian Books is an imprint of Guardian Newspapers Ltd.

A CIP record for this book is available from the British Library.

ISBN: 9-781-4081-0114-8

This book is produced using paper that is made from wood grown in
managed, sustainable forests. It is natural, renewable and recyclable. The
logging and manufacturing processes conform to the environmental
regulations of the country of origin.

Design by Fion
Typeset by Refi
Printed in the United Kingdom by CPI Bookmarque, Croydon

Contents

About the author

Moira O'Neill has been a personal finance journalist for 12 years. Six of these were spent writing articles about saving and investing at *Money Observer* magazine, where she was deputy editor. At the same time, she was also personal finance editor of *Guardian Weekly*, the newspaper for British expatriates. She is currently personal finance editor at the *Investors Chronicle*. She is married and has a three year old daughter.

Disclaimer

About the

Information provided in this book is only for your general information and use and is not intended to address your particular requirements. Independent professional financial advice should be obtained before making any investment decisions.

The value and income derived from investments can go down as well as up. Past performance cannot be relied upon as a guide to future performance.

All facts, figures and other data contained in this book have been obtained from sources believed to be reliable. Although carefully verified by the author, this information cannot be guaranteed by the author.

The author has made every effort to ensure that facts and figures in this book were accurate at the time of writing. However, the financial world changes very quickly and you should check current tax rates and allowances before making financial decisions.

Introduction

If parents weighed up the cost of raising a child, perhaps they would think twice about procreating. From birth to age 21, young Jack and Olivia – the most popular names for children born in 2008 – will cost their parents an eye-watering £194,000.

The aim of this sobering figure (calculated by insurance company LV=) is not to put you off having children in the first place (and, after all, if you're reading this book, it's probably too late). Instead, it is meant to encourage parents, grandparents and other friends or family members to plan ahead. Parents in particular need to make an early start in organising their finances in order to leap these financial hurdles.

Many couples find life difficult enough before children come along. Up until the credit crunch in summer 2007, house prices had soared sky high and many mortgage lenders were approving huge mortgage loans for couples to enable them to get on to the property ladder. If you are in this situation, then money will be tight.

Like most couples, having children wasn't a financial decision for my husband and me. We decided to have a baby and somehow manage, but it hasn't been easy. We both work full time (partly a financial decision) and we juggle our working lives so that our daughter spends as little time in childcare as necessary (again, partly a financial decision as nursery fees are very expensive). I would say that we're comfortable, but we live quite frugally. We don't have a car, for example, and my daughter lives mostly in charity-shop or second-hand clothes. It's all about priorities. This is how we manage to save some money and invest it for our daughter's future and for our own retirement.

The vast majority of parents struggle with money issues at some point. You're never going to be able to do exactly what you want, but this book aims to help you to find the money to save, to prioritise your money goals and to make the important decisions about where to put your cash to give your children a better future.

You'll know that parenthood changes your life dramatically because it brings such huge responsibilities. But have you noticed how it changes the way you think? I no longer focus on day-to-day issues so much. I'm thinking and planning for the long term. Where we live has been a subject of much debate for my husband and me. Should we stay in our flat in London or move to a house outside the M25, for example? We think about where our daughter might go to primary and secondary school. We think about the financial implications of having more children. We even think about retirement.

The trouble is it can be hard for parents to find any spare cash to save in the first place. Then if they do have any money to spare, it's difficult to know what to do with it to help ease these financial burdens. Financial institutions are lining up to give a helping hand to parents who have the resources and foresight to put a little aside each month to alleviate this huge financial burden. But the vast choice means it can be difficult to know where to start.

If your child was born on or after September 2002, then she or he will have a government-sponsored Child Trust Fund. We'll look at Child Trust Funds in depth and also at the other options for saving and investing for children.

Should you put the cash in a savings account? Or invest in the stock market? And in what investment fund? Is it better to use the Child Trust Fund or an individual savings account (ISA)? There have never been so many different choices for parents and others wanting to save and invest for the next generation.

But first you're going to have to take a hard look at your family's finances. You may need to do some streamlining before you can find the money to save.

This book aims to guide you through the financial burden of bringing up children. I'll show you where to find financial help. I'll include information on state help – even relatively well-off families get some cash from the government. And I'll explain how to manage your family's money better.

Then I'll guide you through the confusing world of investments to make sure that your spare cash ends up in the best place to give your children the boost they'll need in five, 10 or 20 years' time.

Finally, I'll give some tips on how to make sure your child builds up a healthy relationship with money.

Reasons to save for children

There are so many reasons to save for children that just thinking about it can be quite overwhelming. Even the small-ticket items such as school uniforms and dance or music lessons can add up to large sums over several years. There will also be occasional big lump-sum items to fund, such as school trips and holidays, or a new bike. However, it is the really big-ticket items such as school and university fees that keep many parents awake at night.

The annual 'Cost of a Child' survey from insurance and investment group LV= (formerly Liverpool Victoria), now in its sixth year, shows that parents could spend £193,772 on raising a child from birth to the age of 21. This is equivalent to £9,227 a year, £769 a month or £25.28 a day.

The survey, by the UK's largest friendly society, shows that the cost of raising a child has increased by 38 per cent over the six years since the survey began in 2003. Childcare and education remain the biggest expenditures, costing parents £53,818 and £50,240.

From a child's birth to age 21, the LV= 'Cost of a Child' survey shows that the average UK household could spend

£17,205 on a child's food, £11,920 on holidays, £13,281 on clothing and £10,313 on hobbies and toys.

Note that the survey does not include the cost of a private education. Not everyone wants to send his or her children to private school. But many who would like to educate their children privately will be put off by the fact that independent school fees are increasing far faster than inflation, with the average day school fee per term nearing £3,000. For more on planning for school fees, turn to Chapter 20.

After a child turns 18, if parents don't throw their offspring into the harsh university of life or school of hard knocks, but allow them to choose the route of higher education, young Jack and Olivia will graduate with massive debts. Funding a university degree is now much more challenging since top-up tuition fees for university students were introduced in England and Wales in September 2006. This means many of them graduate with large debts – and the average student owes £13,500 on graduation. For more on planning for a university education see Chapter 3.

You might think that once your child is out of education, the financial burden ends. But the requests for financial help often continue into young adulthood, with many children asking parents for help to get on to the property ladder, or the more traditional help with wedding costs. They may even continue to live at home during their twenties or even into their thirties. This can be both a blessing and a curse. Marketers call children in this situation KIPPERS, which stands for 'Kids in parents' properties eating into retirement savings'.

Here is a quick breakdown of some of the expensive milestones in your child's life.

Big expenses

	Cost today	Cost in 18 years*
Deposit on first home	£17,600	£27,500
Wedding	£15,900	£24,700
First car	£7,500	£11,700

* *These figures assume inflation of 2.5 per cent a year*
Source: The Children's Mutual

Average costs and debts

- Average student debt on graduation in 2006 was £13,252, according to the National Union of Students.
- Average expected cost of a gap year between school and university is £3,932 (Association of Investment Companies).
- The cost of a typical wedding now rings in at more than £17,000, according to new research from Alliance & Leicester Personal Loans.

- The average deposit for graduate first-time buyers is currently £16,666 (rising to £26,536 in London), according to Scottish Widows Bank.
- Parents of pupils starting private secondary school could pay as much as £140,952 for their secondary school career.

Adult kids

Many parents forego their own financial freedom to support their children into adulthood. Over half of parents (55 per cent) assist adult children with the cost of living, not just with one-off contributions for things such as weddings, and an 'adult child' costs his or her parents £21,540 on average, according to research from LV=.

The study, which was carried out among adults aged 40 years and over who have children aged 18 years and over, found that nine out of ten parents (94 per cent) continue to contribute financially towards education and other major purchases such as houses and cars, plus living expenses, once their children have reached 'adulthood'.

Helping your children financially may be an even longer-lasting affair than you thought. The research also found that 2.3 million 'grandparent' households are financially contributing towards two generations – their children and their grandchildren. Almost half (46 per cent) of over 70s are still supporting their children financially, despite generally being retired.

But it wasn't like this in your parents' day. Less than one third (29 per cent) of today's parents received financial support from their parents after they left school.

What parents help with financially	What parents spend on average
First home	**£5,602** 63% of parents have contributed more than £3,000 towards their adult child's first home, with 31% contributing more than £9,000.
Savings and investments	**£3,340** 64% have contributed more than £1,000 towards their adult children's savings and investments, with 22% donating more than £5,000.
First car	**£1,702** 42% of parents contribute more than £1,000 to the cost of their child's first car, with 15% of parents contributing more than £3,000.
Wedding	**£3,111** 19% contributed more than £5,000 towards their child's wedding.

University fees	**£2,245 per year, totalling £6,735** (based on a three-year degree course) 21% of parents spend more than £3,000 a year on their child's university fees.
Travelling	**£1,050** 25% of parents contributed more than £1,000 towards their adult child's travel costs.
Total	**£21,540***

* This does not include contributions towards general living costs, which 55 per cent of parents admitted to helping their adult children with, or other costs that parents may contribute towards.

Not yet 'flown the nest'

Nearly one quarter (23 per cent) of parents aged between 40 and 49 years still have children aged over 25 years old living with them, indicating that despite falling house prices, adult children are not in a hurry to leave the nest, and may not be able to afford to either.

The study shows that parents can no longer expect their children to pay their own way once they have actually left. More than ever, it's true to say that having children means signing up to a lifetime of financial commitment.

All figures, unless otherwise stated, are from YouGov Research. Total sample size was 1,184 adults aged 40 years and above with at least one child aged 18 years or over. Fieldwork was undertaken between 5 and 6 June 2008.

2 Money and your family

Having children changes the way you think about money. Issues that many not have been on your radar before, such as financial security and planning for the future, become your priority.

Many couples will find that being parents brings very different challenges from those of DINKYs (double income no kids yet). There will be many decisions to make, such as should you go back to work, or work full time? What kind of lifestyle do you want to provide for your kids? Should you sacrifice your own financial goals, such as a comfortable retirement, for the sake of the children? These decisions are not easy and there is no right answer. You will have to learn to compromise.

If money was no object, seven out of ten working parents would have stayed at home to raise their children, according to a YouGov survey of 4,330 adults, conducted for uSwitch between 18 and 21 February 2008. However, the choice of caring for your own children is rapidly turning into a luxury available only to those who can afford it.

According to the Office for National Statistics, there were 2.8 million stay-at-home parents in 1993, compared to

2.2 million in 2008. This is a decrease of 21 per cent – the lowest level in 15 years. The YouGov survey for uSwitch revealed that the cost of living has pushed over one million new parents back to work.

Single parents may find decision-making easier – as there is no partner to argue with – but may struggle for other reasons, such as having only one income and less flexibility as there is no partner to help with childcare.

My experience

When I got married, my husband and I decided to wait for a few months before trying for a baby in order to put some money aside to make us feel more secure. I put this into a tax-free individual savings account (more on these in Chapter 13). When I found out that I was pregnant, I started increasing these savings to get a pot of money to tide me through maternity leave and pay for some essential baby things.

When our daughter, Eleanor, was born, I took a year's maternity leave from my full-time job because I wanted to spend as much time as possible with my baby. I knew that I was going to return to work full time at the end of this period as I was the main breadwinner for our family.

The thought of leaving my baby in childcare caused me a lot of heartache. But on the day I returned to work,

I realised that I had made the right decision as I love my job and it is a huge part of my identity. I also liked the idea of being able to provide for myself and secure a comfortable future for our family. I place a high value on financial security. Fortunately, my employer allowed me to work flexibly, which meant I could juggle my hours to spend one afternoon mid-week with my daughter. The other days of the week I started work an hour earlier than my colleagues to compensate for the missing afternoon.

In the run-up to going back to work, many issues came up. My husband and I didn't always see eye to eye. After having a baby, I wanted to move to a larger property with a garden, which would mean living in a less expensive area. He wanted to stay in our flat in a good area of North London, near a highly-regarded primary school. He argued that taking on a large mortgage would make us sacrifice our standard of living. We wouldn't be able to go on nice holidays, for example. Until we both earned substantially more, we decided not to move.

Then we had to decide what childcare to use. The decision was relatively simple as none of the local childminders had spaces for our daughter and we couldn't afford a nanny. We settled on a pleasant nursery quite near to our home and on our commute to work. But monthly fees of £1,200 (in London, nursery fees are much higher than in the rest of the country) were eating up most of my husband's take-home salary.

We discussed whether he should be a stay-at-home dad, but he didn't want to do this. So we decided that there would be a few tough years when we would be forking out huge sums on childcare but that hopefully a seamless work history would pay off for him in better-paid jobs and opportunities in future. This soon turned out to be a smart decision financially, as when our daughter was two he found a much better paid job. Our dream house now seems less of a dream and, although we're not yet in a position to move up the ladder, that prospect seems nearer.

If we have another child, then everything might change again. What I've learnt is that parenting brings unique financial pressures. And those financial decisions are also very emotional ones. What might be right for someone else may not be right for you. And you have to learn how to make those decisions as a couple. Not everyone finds it easy. In fact money issues are often the main source of trouble within relationships.

We don't have much spare cash, but we do manage to save a little for our daughter each month. I'm putting it into the stock market in the hope that it will have grown to a tidy sum when she reaches 18. In the meantime, I also try to save some money in a cash account so that we can have family treats every now and then.

We're lucky in that, when Eleanor was born, her grandfather wanted to contribute to a savings scheme for her future education. We learnt this in a roundabout way. My mother said: 'Your dad would like to do something for baby Ella, but he's too embarrassed to ask.' We had likewise been too embarrassed to broach the subject. Now he contributes to her Child Trust Fund (CTF), although we took the decision on what fund to invest in (more on CTFs in Chapter 12).

I find myself thinking about what my daughter will face in future, particularly as a young adult. I don't think life will be easy for her, so I want her to have a good start. I'd rather put a little money aside for her future than dress her in designer clothes. I'd like to be able to give her enough of a nest egg to pay her way through university and hopefully help her on to the housing ladder with a deposit. My father did this for me and I'll be forever grateful to him.

We're putting aside money in tens and hundreds, rather than thousands, but I know that in the long run even small amounts saved now will grow to decent sums to start her adult life. I try not to spend as much on myself as I did before having children. And what I do buy is often in a sale or second-hand.

I doubt that we will educate her privately but, who knows, this may change. I have a friend who has gone back to work specifically to earn the money to send her son to private school, where she believes he will be much happier.

State help for your family

Until you become a parent you are probably unaware of how much state help there is for families with children. The UK is not as family friendly as some other countries in Europe, where there is state-subsidised childcare for all, for example. But there is still plenty of state help available, even for relatively wealthy families. Don't ignore what is on offer, as even small amounts added to your child's savings pot can add up to big sums in the long run.

The government's Ten Year Childcare Strategy, *Choice for Parents: The Best Start for Children*, was published alongside the Pre-Budget Report on 2 December 2004. Its key themes were:

■ **choice and flexibility** – greater choice for parents in how they balance their work commitments and family life through enhanced parental leave and easy access to Sure Start children's centres for all;

■ **availability** – flexible childcare for all families with children aged up to 14 who need it; and 15 hours a week free early education for all three- and four-year-olds for 38 weeks a year, with 20 hours as a goal;

■ **quality** – high-quality provision delivered by a skilled early years and childcare workforce, with full daycare settings professionally led and a strengthened qualification and career structure; and

- **affordability** – affordable provision appropriate to their needs with substantial increases in tax credit support.

Current State help for parents includes:

Maternity and paternity leave

If you're a couple where both partners work, the first thing to do when your baby's arrival is imminent is to check what maternity and paternity leave you are entitled to. Having paid time off work when a baby is born is an enormous benefit to your family's finances. It can be the lifeline that gets you through this crucial period when money is very tight. There are minimum state entitlements for both types of leave.

Maternity leave and pay

If you are a mother who is an employee, you have the statutory right to a minimum amount of maternity leave. Statutory Maternity Leave is for 52 weeks. You may be entitled to receive Statutory Maternity Pay (SMP) for up to 39 weeks of the leave.

Your employer may also have their own scheme which could be more generous than the statutory scheme. Check your contract of employment or staff handbook for details, or ask your employer. Your employer can't offer you less than the statutory scheme.

As an employee, you have the right to 26 weeks of

Ordinary Maternity Leave and 26 weeks' Additional Maternity Leave – making one year in total. Provided you meet certain notification requirements, you can take this regardless of long you've been with your employer and no matter how many hours you work or how much you're paid. You continue to be an employee throughout your Ordinary and Additional Maternity Leave.

While you're on Ordinary Maternity Leave, you keep your normal employment rights and benefits (apart from wages). These might include access to a company car or mobile phone that you have as part of your employment contract. If you take Additional Maternity Leave, some contractual rights and benefits (e.g. company car) can be suspended, although your statutory rights continue.

For babies that arrived on or after 5 October 2008, the mothers keep their normal employment rights and benefits (apart from wages) throughout their Ordinary and Additional Maternity Leave.

The maternity pay benefits you might get will vary depending on your circumstances. Usually you will claim either statutory or contractual maternity pay from your employer or Maternity Allowance (MA) through Jobcentre Plus or a Jobs and Benefits office in Northern Ireland.

To qualify for Statutory Maternity Pay, you must have been:

- employed by the same employer continuously (some breaks do not interrupt continuous employment) for at least 26 weeks into the fifteenth week before the week your baby is due; and
- earning an average of at least £90 a week (before tax).

To claim Statutory Maternity Pay, you must tell your employer at least 28 days before the date you want the pay to start from. Your employer may require you to inform them in writing.

If you get SMP, your employer will pay you 90 per cent of your average weekly earnings for the first six weeks, then up to £117.18 a week for the remaining 33 weeks. This isn't a great deal, but it is certainly enough to cover nappies, clothes and other items for your baby, plus maybe some of the household food bills and a portion of the mortgage or rent.

You pay tax and National Insurance on Statutory Maternity Pay in the same way as on your regular wages. Your employer reclaims the majority of SMP from their National Insurance contributions (NICs) and other payments. To qualify for SMP, you must pay tax and National Insurance as an employee (or would pay if you earned enough or are old enough).

Maternity Allowance

If you can't get SMP from your employer, you might get Maternity Allowance if you:

- are employed;
- are self-employed and pay Class 2 National Insurance contributions or have a Small Earnings Exception Certificate; or
- are not employed but have worked close to or during your pregnancy.

The conditions are that you must:

- have been employed or self-employed for at least 26 of the 66 weeks before the week your baby was due (a part week counts as a full week); and
- earned an average of £30 over any 13 of those 66 weeks.

The standard rate of MA is £117.18 or 90 per cent of your average weekly earnings, whichever is less. MA is paid for up to 39 weeks; it is not liable to income tax or National Insurance contributions.

Other family benefits you may be entitled to

There are a number of additional benefits available to expectant and new mothers. These include Sure Start Maternity Grants and free prescriptions and dental treatment and tax credits. Whether you qualify for these benefits will depend on your personal situation. Visit www.direct.gov.uk for more information on these.

Paternity leave and pay

If you are a father-to-be or you'll be responsible, together with the mother, for bringing up the child, you have the right to paid paternity leave, providing you meet certain conditions (see the Direct Gov website, www.direct.gov.uk, for information).

If you are eligible for paid paternity leave, you can take either one or two weeks for your leave. You can't take odd days off and if you take two weeks they must be taken together. You can choose to start the leave:

- on the day the baby's born;
- a number of days or weeks after the baby's born; or
- from a specific date after the first day of the week in which the baby's expected to be born.

Your leave can start on any day of the week (but not before the baby is born), but it has to finish within 56 days of the baby being born or, if the baby's born before the week it was due, within 56 days of the first day of that week.

If your average weekly earnings are £90 or more (before tax), Statutory Paternity Pay is paid for one or two consecutive weeks at £117.18, or 90 per cent of your average weekly earnings if this is less.

Some employers have their own paternity leave arrangements – check your contract of employment. You can always choose the statutory arrangement if this suits you better. Rights to paternity leave are extra to your normal holiday allowance.

Child Benefit

Child Benefit is a tax-free payment that all parents can claim for their child. It is usually paid every four weeks, but in some cases can be paid weekly, and there are separate rates for each child. The payment can be claimed by anyone who qualifies, whatever their income or savings.

There are two separate amounts, with a higher amount for your eldest (or only) child. In the tax year 2009/10, Child Benefit is £20 a week for your oldest child and £13.20 a week for each of your other children. This may not sound like a huge amount, but it's over £1,000 a year for the oldest child, which is almost enough to fully fund the government-sponsored Child Trust Fund which all children receive at birth.

Child Benefit is intended to help pay for the upkeep of your child. It will certainly help with the cost of shoes and school uniforms. But many parents who can afford to get by without it treat it as a bonus payment that can be used to invest on behalf of a child.

Investing your Child Benefit from day one is a great way to get the savings ball rolling – and you won't miss the money if you stash it away before you have a chance to get used to the extra cash in your pocket.

If you need further convincing that putting a relatively small amount away each month will be worth it, here's the proof. In November 2007, the *Guardian* asked investment house M&G to establish whether investing Child Benefit payments could produce enough to cover the entire cost of sending a child to university.

Taking estimates of living costs from various universities around the country, plus typical tuition fees of £3,075 a year, the study estimated that a three-year undergraduate course starting in 2007 would cost at least £30,000. Looking back at the Child Benefit rates for the previous 18 years, M&G worked out that parents would have received an average of £53.80 per month for an eldest child who is now 18 – amounting to £11,620.80 in benefits. If, throughout those 18 years, they had invested that £53.80 each month in a building society savings account, it would have grown to £14,064 after deduction of basic-rate tax.

If, however, they had invested the monthly sum in equities, which have historically outperformed other types of investments over periods of ten years or more, and had chosen to put it in the M&G Recovery fund, they would be looking at a return of £32,701 after tax – more than enough to cover the total cost of university.

The *Guardian* asked another large and long-established investment fund, the Foreign & Colonial Investment Trust, to run the same calculation. It found that a sum of £53.80 per month for the 18 years to 2007 invested in the trust would have grown to £30,086.91 after tax.

Child Benefit can be paid into any bank, building society or National Savings & Investments (NS&I) account that accepts direct payment. It's usually paid every four weeks, but it can be paid weekly if you're getting Income Support or Income-based Jobseeker's Allowance or if you're a single parent.

The only way to claim Child Benefit is to fill in a Child Benefit claim form and send it to the Child Benefit Office along with your child's birth or adoption certificate. You can't claim over the phone or via the Internet.

There are several ways of getting a claim form. You can:

- get one from the 'Bounty Pack' that's given to new mothers in hospital;
- fill in a Child Benefit claim form online at www.hmrc.gov.uk and print it out, although you'll still have to post it to the Child Benefit Office;

- print out a blank Child Benefit claim form from www.hmrc.gov.uk and fill it in by hand;
- if you have problems getting a claim form, contact the Child Benefit Helpline on 0845 302 1444.

Make sure you apply for Child Benefit as soon as your baby is born because HM Revenue & Customs (HMRC) can only backdate your Child Benefit for up to three months from the date they get your claim. It is also important to apply for Child Benefit straight away, as the application automatically triggers the child's right to a Child Trust Fund voucher. This voucher from the government is worth £250 and must be invested until the child turns 18 in a tax-free Child Trust Fund (for more details turn to Chapter 12).

How claiming Child Benefit can protect your State Pension

Another important reason to claim Child Benefit is that it can protect your rights to a State Pension. The basic State Pension in tax year 2009/10 is £95.25 a week from age 65. If you are under 50, it is not possible to know what it might be worth when you reach retirement, but it's probably going to be a decent enough sum – and you don't want to miss out.

So if you're at home looking after children, or you're a working parent who doesn't earn enough to pay National Insurance contributions (NICs), there's a scheme to protect your State Pension. This is called 'Home Responsibilities Protection' (HRP) and it can protect your State Pension entitlement if you get Child Benefit.

HRP isn't a benefit but a way of safeguarding how much State Pension you'll get. Your State Pension is based on the number of 'qualifying years' you build up during your working life. A qualifying year is one when you earn enough to pay NICs, so if you're not working or not earning enough to pay NICs, your pension could suffer.

HRP stops you losing out if you're caring for children. It does this by reducing the number of qualifying years you need to get a State Pension. Each full tax year when you get Child Benefit for a child under 16 reduces the number of qualifying years you need.

Only the person who claims and receives Child Benefit can get HRP. Therefore, if you are married or in a civil partnership or living with your partner, it's important to decide together whose pension most needs protecting. The person you decide on is the one who should claim Child Benefit. It's likely to be the one who stays at home to look after the children. For further information about HRP, visit www.directgov.uk.

Tax credits

Your family may qualify for financial help from means-tested tax credits. Make sure you investigate this option fully as, according to HMRC, nine out of ten families with children are entitled to tax credits.

A family might be entitled to one or both of Child Tax Credit and Working Tax Credit, The money acknowledges and supports the costs of bringing up children and can substantially boost the income of even relatively well-off families.

Families on incomes of up to £58,175 a year (or £66,350 a year if there is at least one child who is less than a year old) can benefit from Child Tax Credit, whether or not they are working. Parents can follow a simple guide on the Directgov website (www.direct.gov.uk) to see whether they are eligible for tax credits. Further information is available on the HMRC website, including a number of leaflets which can be viewed online or downloaded as PDFs.

Also, the Tax Credit Helpline (tel. 0845 300 3900) provides information and helps parents to complete their claim form or check the progress of their claim.

Child Tax Credit

Child Tax Credit is for people who are responsible for at least one child or qualifying young person. Child Tax Credit is paid direct to the person who is mainly responsible for caring for the child or children.

The payment is made up of two elements: a family element paid to any family with at least one child and worth up to £545 a year; and a child element paid for each child in the family and worth up to £2,085 in 2008/09. Parents might get more if they have a child under one or a disabled child.

Child Tax Credit is paid into the bank account of the main carer – the person who is mainly responsible for looking after the child or children.

Working Tax Credit

Working Tax Credit is for people, including working parents, who earn low wages. You need to be employed or self-employed (either on your own as a sole trader or in a partnership) and usually work 16 hours or more a week. It is paid to the person who is working 16 hours or more a week.

You cannot receive Working Tax Credit if you are not working. If both parents are working 16 hours or more a week, you must choose which one of you will receive it.

As part of Working Tax Credit you may qualify for help towards the costs of childcare. You can get back up to 80 per cent of your costs for eligible childcare up to a maximum of £175 per week. If you receive the childcare element of Working Tax Credit, this will always be paid direct to the person who is mainly responsible for caring for the child or children, alongside payments of Child Tax Credit.

Childcare vouchers (from employers)

Childcare vouchers are a government initiative to help working parents pay for childcare such as childminders, nurseries and play schemes. Parents and their employers will benefit from running a childcare voucher scheme.

Parents save money because childcare vouchers are exempt from tax and National Insurance. The maximum yearly saving for a higher rate taxpayer is £1,195 per parent, so if both parents take childcare vouchers they can save up to £2,390 a year on childcare costs. Basic rate taxpayers can save up to £962 a year.

Employers who run a childcare voucher scheme will pay a lower amount of Employer National Insurance, saving up to £373 for every employee on the scheme. To implement a childcare voucher scheme, employers simply sign up their organisation and then place an order for their participating employees for each pay period.

Be aware that if you sign up for childcare vouchers, this may affect your ability to claim tax credits. Childcare vouchers are not treated as being a payment by you for childcare, which means that receiving childcare vouchers will reduce the childcare costs that your Working Tax Credit calculation is based on, even if you reduce your salary and receive childcare vouchers instead (known as 'salary sacrifice').

Money saving tips for parents

Money saving can start even before the birth of a child. If you're a first-time parent, try not to splash out on lots of baby clothes and equipment before the birth. Once the baby arrives you'll probably find that your family and friends give you lots of gifts and you may end up with two of some items.

Before the birth

Talk to family members and friends who already have children. Ask them what items they found really useful and what they could have done without. This will help you spend your money wisely – and sparingly.

Not everyone will feel comfortable with this idea, but you may want to give family and friends a present wish list so that everyone doesn't buy the same thing. Let people know that you'll welcome used baby clothes and equipment. Some people may be shy of offering them, assuming that you won't want cast-offs.

After the birth

Saving money doesn't always mean going without. Here are some simple cost-cutting tips for the early years. And any money you save can be invested wisely for the future when your children will appreciate it most.

Nappies

Among essential items, these are one of the greatest expenses of having babies. The cheapest way to cut the cost of nappies is to potty train your child early. But this depends on whether the child is ready for it.

The major choice is, of course, between the convenience of shoving soiled disposable nappies in the bin, and shoving reusables in the washing machine. Putting aside the environmental arguments, reusable nappies are generally cheaper in the long term than disposables. You will save even more per child if you have several children and reuse the same ones throughout. The website www.moneysavingexpert.com points out that the ease of one is balanced by the cost savings of the other. Over the two and half years that your child is in nappies, you'd pay roughly £900 on disposables and £400 on reusables – that's a major financial difference.

If you invested £500 in the stock market when your child was two and this earned seven per cent on average each year, then you would have £1,476 (according to the Motley Fool's investment calculator at www.fool.co.uk) by the time your child is 18. That's enough to buy a first car (albeit a bit of an old banger) or a round-the-world airline ticket.

You will need to do some research on different types of reusable nappies and the prices. Also check if your local council offers cash incentives to parents who choose reusable nappies.

If you are using disposables, be conscious that shops' own-brand nappies can be cheaper than leading brands such as Huggies and Pampers. Buying in bulk can also save you money, as can the parenting clubs run by some retailers.

Baby food

Two points here. Breast feeding a baby (if you're able to) is free, while bottle feeding can cost hundreds of pounds. Making your own baby food is much cheaper – and often better tasting – than pre-packaged baby food.

Clothes, toys and equipment

Your baby won't care if he or she wears designer clothes, has the best-looking buggy or top-of-the range toys. Swallow some of your pride and reap the financial rewards of buying baby stuff second-hand. This is particularly relevant if you aren't receiving cast-offs from family and friends.

We saved hundreds of pounds by buying our daughter's clothes in charity shops. While I was on maternity leave I visited the local charity shops every Monday afternoon and built up a wardrobe of clothes, not just for when she was a baby but also for the years ahead when she was four or five.

Online auction sites such as www.ebay.com are the obvious places to search for cheap, second-hand clothes, toys and equipment. They also allow you to make some money back by reselling all these items when you no longer need them.

Things not to buy second-hand

For safety reasons, baby and child car seats should never be bought second-hand. Unless you know the seat's full history it may no longer be safe because it may have been involved in an accident.

Lesser-known money-saving options

Here are some other less well-known money-saving alternatives.

The **Freecycle Network** offers an environmentally-friendly way to cut the cost of the patter of tiny feet and keeps working as your children grow. Set up in 2003, www.freecycle.org is a recycling network initiative where people offer goods they no longer want completely free. You can put in requests for specific items. The babywear section is particularly buoyant. You could pick up a Moses basket, baby sling and all sorts of other kit, saving hundreds of pounds. As your child grows, you may be able to find bicycles, bunk beds and other useful items.

The **National Childbirth Trust** is best known for its range of support services for parents, but its local networks also hold hundreds of nearly-new sales every year, all over the UK. You can pick up children's clothes, toys and equipment very cheaply. Visit www.nct.org.uk for more information.

Your local library may have a toy section through which you can borrow all sorts of toys for free or a minimal charge. This is a great way to find out which toys your child prefers to play with before buying them yourself. That way you avoid wasting money on toys that will sit in the toy box gathering dust.

Babysitting

You can save lots of money on childcare by joining or setting up a babysitting circle with local friends who also have young children. By trading babysitting duties with other parents, you can save £20 to £30 every time you want a night out.

There are many ways of setting up a babysitting circle. Some groups have complicated set-ups, with credits per hour, per child and extra after midnight, but it can be as simple as one credit per babysit.

Cut the costs of childcare

The Daycare Trust's 2008 'Childcare Costs Survey', which examines the costs of nurseries, childminders and out-of-school clubs, revealed that the costs of sending a child to daycare have risen at a rate far exceeding the rate of inflation.

The average cost of a full-time nursery place for a child under two in England is £159 per week, rising to £202 in London and the South East. A childminder costs around £144. Comparing these sums to average earnings of £457 per week makes you realise just how expensive childcare has become.

In England the cost of sending a two year old to a typical nursery increased at a rate of more than double inflation (around five per cent). Parents will feel the pain of these rises, particularly as so many employers have been giving so-called 'cost of living' pay rises of only two or three per cent. Add on recent huge hikes in the cost of energy, fuel, food bills and mortgage rates, and a massive amount of our disposable income is being eaten up every month.

One of the biggest rises discovered by the Daycare Trust is in the cost of after-school clubs. These schemes, which help working parents with school age children, have raised their costs by six times the rate of inflation, now typically costing £43 for 15 hours a week.

The UK's childcare expenses are much higher than those in the rest of Europe, but although the government is trying to persuade parents to combine working with bringing up a family, it hasn't created many solutions to the problem.

Simple maths reveals just how expensive childcare can be: £70 per day (the cost of some nursery places in inner London) is £17,500 per year, with a two-week closure over Christmas. Take into account income tax, and a working parent in London has to earn £25,000 per year just to cover the nursery fees. Many parents feel there is little point in going back to work if what is left after paying for childcare doesn't cover running a car or your monthly bus pass to get you to work, let alone contributing to a mortgage. Furthermore, nursery hours run from 8am to 6pm, so if you have an hour's commute to work, that leaves only jobs where the hours of work are 9am to 5pm, with no chance of staying late to attend a meeting or evening function.

Many parents somehow manage to make the maths work when they have one child. But with two or more children, the sums may be more than you can handle. Two kids in nursery means two sets of fees. Even assuming some sibling discount, the bill could reach £30,000 a year, which requires a gross annual salary of £42,000 just to cover it.

Hiring a nanny may seem a cheaper option if you are a family with more than one child. But the problem here is that you are hit by a double tax bill. You have to pay the nanny's salary out of your own after-tax salary, plus as an employer you have to pay the nanny's National Insurance contributions as well.

A qualified nanny with decent experience will cost you £400 per week after tax, which equals £600 per week including tax, or £31,200 per year. That's not very different from nursery fees for two children. Note that you also have to cover holiday pay and find emergency cover if the nanny is sick, which doesn't apply to a nursery – it will open most weeks of the year.

Ways to cut the cost

Many working parents juggle their working hours to cut the cost of childcare. Others have free childcare from family members, for example grandparents, which helps a huge amount with family finances.

Aside from these options, there are a few schemes that might help.

- **Tax credits**. If your family income is below £58,175 per year (£66,350 if you have a child under one) you may be able to claim Child Tax Credit or Working Tax Credit. The government estimates that nine out of ten families are entitled to claim tax credits, which provide help with childcare costs.

- **Free part-time early years places**. This scheme is available to all three and four year olds (the year before they start school) and gives up to 12.5 hours (increasing to 15 hours in 2010) of childcare for free, for 38 weeks of the year.
- **Childcare Vouchers scheme**. Parents who are employed may find that their employer has signed up to the childcare vouchers scheme. This allows parents to sacrifice some of their gross salary in return for 'vouchers' that can be used to pay for childcare. The first £55 of childcare each week (£243 each month) can be bought free of tax or National Insurance, meaning a lower rate taxpayer could save around £962 per year, and a higher rate taxpayer around £1,195. In London, that will just about cover one month's full-time nursery fees for one child. However, if you are able to claim benefits, you may find the Childcare Vouchers scheme affects these, so do some research before signing up.
- Some large companies also offer their staff subsidised on-site crèche facilities.

My experience

My husband and I juggled our working hours to cut down on the costs of childcare – and to ensure that our daughter doesn't do a full week in nursery. My husband is off on Fridays but works Sundays and I manage to have a half day mid-week with my daughter.

We found that council-run nurseries in our area are much cheaper than the expensive private nursery that we first sent our daughter to (an eye-watering £70 a day). But you have to get on to a waiting list for nurseries run by councils – fortunately we managed to get her into one when she turned two and the cost is now a much more reasonable £35 a day, plus the staff are much more caring and dedicated.

Getting your family priorities right

Saving and investing for your children has to be put in the context of your whole family's finances – for example, paying the mortgage and putting money aside to ensure a comfortable retirement. If you are a young couple starting out on low incomes, or a single parent, then it may not be possible to put aside huge amounts of money for the kids.

There are lots of financial planning elements that ought to be in place before you can even think about starting to put aside extra money for your children.

Importance of an emergency cash fund

What would you do if you lost your job? Could your family survive? And for how long? Do you want to risk losing your house through defaulting on your mortgage repayments? How would you cope if you had an expensive family emergency? Imagine your teenage daughter were to go on a round-the-world trip and fall off a moped in Thailand, resulting in a trip to hospital. Unless your daughter had the appropriate travel insurance, you would have to fly her back home at great expense. What would you do if the car and the washing machine broke down in the same month?

There are many reasons to build an emergency cash fund and this MUST be your financial priority. It will keep you afloat if something unexpected crops up. Financial advisers recommend that you put aside at least three months' – preferably six months' – salary in an easy-access cash account. If you have many financial dependents, you may feel more comfortable with a larger emergency cash fund – perhaps the equivalent of a year's salary.

However, make sure that the money in your cash fund is working as hard as it can. Many banks and building society accounts pay rubbish rates of interest. You must find one that pays more than the current rate of inflation, measured by the Retail Prices Index (RPI), otherwise your money is losing its value.

Cash accounts usually take off 20 per cent of the interest as savings tax. So if your account pays 5 per cent interest, you will only receive 4 per cent. And if RPI inflation is 3 per cent, then your deposit is only really growing at 1 per cent a year.

Your best option is to put as much of your emergency cash fund as possible in a cash individual savings account (ISA) where it will probably get a top rate of interest, plus avoid the 20 per cent savings tax. These are available from most banks and building societies. You can check the best rates on cash ISAs in the personal finance pages of national newspapers or at websites such as www.moneyfacts.co.uk.

Not all cash ISAs are easily accessible though, so when you're looking for a home for your emergency fund, check how long it will take to access your money. You can put a maximum of £3,600 a year into a cash ISA so it may take a few years to transfer all your emergency fund over. But couples have double the allowance, so you may want to put some of your funds into a cash ISA for your partner. In the meantime, you can keep the surplus monies in a normal bank or building society account, but make sure you're getting a decent rate.

Get the right financial protection

On the whole, most people's financial priorities are misguided. You probably worry more about losing your mobile phone than how you would cope financially if you had a critical illness. If you have a family, it is time to face up to your own mortality – very difficult to do. However, insuring your possessions should not be prioritised above insuring your own health and life.

Income protection insurance: Cinderella of insurance policies

Protecting your income is more important than saving for your children as, without an income, you won't be able to build up a savings pot. This is where insurance comes into play, particularly income protection insurance, though you may also need life insurance and critical illness insurance.

The one thing that pays for everything else – your income – is often the last thing people insure. Make sure this isn't the case and protect yourself and your family by taking out income protection insurance.

An income protection insurance policy gives you a regular tax-free income if you are injured or too ill to work. It is the best-kept secret of the financial services industry. You may not have heard of this type of insurance as it is not nearly as well promoted as life insurance or its ugly sister payment protection insurance.

However, an average man under 50 is twice as likely to be off work for more than six months because of an accident or sickness than he is to die. Bear in mind that if you are seriously disabled, your living costs are likely to rise to enable you to cope with your disability.

If you have a family and children, income protection is often viewed as more important than life insurance. Think through the impact of your death compared to illness or disability: if you die, your family will miss your income. However, if you are seriously ill or disabled, your family not only loses your income but also has to find extra money to support you. In blunt terms, you are a more expensive liability to your family if you are injured or seriously ill than if you die.

Make sure you get the right type of income protection. Don't confuse real income protection with the inferior payment protection insurance, which is usually sold alongside loans, mortgages and credit cards. This type of policy will only pay out an income for a maximum of one to two years, and often has clauses in the policy that enable the insurer to refuse to pay out, for stress related-illnesses, for example. It does, however, have its place if you can't get income protection because of poor health – payment protection does not require medical underwriting.

A real income protection policy is sometimes known as permanent health insurance and continues to pay out until you are well enough to return to work, reach retirement age or die – whichever happens first.

What you need to know about income protection

- An income protection policy is fully underwritten, which means you will be asked many personal and medical questions on application. The price you pay will depend on your age, sex, general health (including whether you smoke) and employment status. Those in professional, office-based jobs generally pay less than those in physically demanding jobs.

- It is best to take out an 'own occupation' policy, so that if you can't do your current job you can claim. Some policies are written on inferior 'any occupation' terms, which means you would be forced to take up other perhaps less desirable or lower-status employment if your health permitted.

- A full income protection policy is sometimes known as permanent health insurance.

- Income protection is generally more expensive than payment protection, but you are getting a far superior and much better-value policy. If you want to cut the price of income protection, you can lengthen the time period after which the policy starts to pay out. Some policies pay out as soon as you become ill or suffer a disability, but you could change this to a year or two years after you become seriously ill or disabled. You need to ensure you have enough savings to last until the policy pays out.

- The maximum monthly benefit is usually a tax-free payment equal to around 65 per cent of your gross income.

- Policy wordings differ and there are important rules and conditions attached to policies. For this reason, it is very important that you seek independent financial advice before taking out income protection insurance.

Important note for employees

Before taking out a policy, check if your employer covers you. If you work for a large organisation it is very likely that your employer provides you with some form of income protection through the company insurance scheme. Check what level of cover is provided, though, as many company schemes only pay out for six months. If this is the case, you need to top up your protection with private insurance.

Number crunching

You are 26 times more likely to be incapacitated and off work for more than six months than you are to die before the age of 65 (source: Norwich Union). Only nine per cent of people have an income protection policy sufficient to cover their outgoings, should they lose their income (source: Alliance & Leicester).

What you get from the state

Some people are happy to rely on the state and, for such people, income protection is not suitable. However, be aware that state help is very thin on the ground. Following a change of government policy in 2008, there is a small amount of state help to pay your mortgage if you lose your job, but this may not last for long.

People who can't work through illness or disability may be able to receive Incapacity Benefit, a weekly payment for people under the State Pension age. For the first 28 weeks off work, you could be eligible for £63.75 a week. For weeks 29 to 52, the payment rises to £75.40. The long-term rate paid for absences over 53 weeks is £84.50 (2008/09 figures).

Other benefits may include Housing Benefit or a reduction in council tax. However, for anyone with a family to support, these won't stretch far.

Life insurance: only if you have financial dependants

If you have financial dependants, such as children, life insurance is essential. Life insurance pays a lump sum if you die during the term of the policy.

Critical illness cover pays a lump sum if you are diagnosed with a life-threatening condition such as cancer or heart disease. They are sometimes combined in the same policy.

With both types of insurance, premiums increase as you get older and you'll pay more if you have health problems that reduce your life expectancy.

Family income benefit

This is often the most cost-effective type of family protection. It's a form of life insurance, but rather than providing a lump sum should you die, family income benefit provides a regular, tax-free monthly income for you and your dependants – from the time of the claim to the end of the plan term.

For example, if the plan term is 20 years and the claim is made after 16 years, benefits will be paid for the remaining four years. This is why family income benefit often costs less than life insurance.

Family income benefit is particularly attractive to those who like to know they have a regular monthly income and would rather not have to worry about complex investment decisions to make the most of a lump sum payout.

Importance of making a will

Everyone should make a will, particularly if you have children. But not many people do. Just one in three people in the UK have a will prepared (according to research from Barclays Wealth). However, a will is one of the easiest ways to protect your wealth and the only way to be sure that your wishes are fulfilled. They also avoid any misunderstandings.

Four good reasons to make a will

1. **You decide who benefits**. Without a will, the law decides who benefits. Therefore, if you fail to make a will, the people to whom you would like to leave your estate may receive little or nothing at all, and others may benefit who you did not wish to do so.

2. **You can appoint guardians for your children**. Terrible accidents do occur and responsible parents should consider what would happen to their children if they were not there. It is possible to appoint guardians who

will be responsible for your children's upbringing if neither parent is alive. You can also appoint someone you trust to look after your assets until the children are old enough to take responsibility for themselves.

3. **You can ensure your partner inherits**. Unmarried partners and partners who have not registered a civil partnership cannot inherit from each other unless there is a will.

4. **Your beneficiaries pay less inheritance tax**. It may be possible to reduce the amount of tax payable on a large inheritance if advice is taken in advance and a will is made.

Dying without a will

If you die without making a will, you die 'intestate' and your estate will be distributed according to the Law on Intestacy. It does not matter what you may have wished for or promised while you were alive. The law decides who gets what.

The intestacy rules could leave your family struggling to survive financially. They could also mean that your wealth is passed to family members that you might not have wanted to be included. Friends get nothing under the laws of intestacy – again, something that you might not be happy about.

If you have no will, it may well surprise you to hear that your husband or wife does not automatically inherit all your estate. Here is what happens under the law in England

and Wales (there are different laws in Scotland and Ireland), depending on your family circumstances.

- **Married with children**. By law, a surviving spouse receives the chattels (your goods and personal belongings), the first £250,000 and a life interest in half of the rest. The children receive the other half of the residue in equal shares.
- **Married without children**. Your spouse gets the first £450,000, plus half of the balance. The remaining half goes to your other relatives in this order of priority: parents, brothers/sisters, half brothers/sisters, grandparents, aunts/uncles.
- **Not married, with children**. Your estate will be shared equally between the children. Should they die before you, then their children would take their share.
- **Not married, without children, with relatives**. Your estate will be shared among relatives in this order of priority: parents, brothers/sisters, half brothers/sisters, grandparents, aunts/uncles.
- **Not married and have no relatives**. Your whole estate goes to the Crown.

The Law on Intestacy does not recognise a 'common law' wife or husband, but it does recognise a civil partner. If you are not legally married and your other half dies, you get nothing, although if you can prove that you were financially dependent on the deceased, you may be able to apply for provision from the estate. However, this can be costly, time consuming and may not necessarily be successful.

If a divorce is finalised before the death, the marriage is over and the divorced spouse gets nothing.

Except for spouses, only blood relatives inherit. If, for instance, a brother would have inherited a share but died first, his widow would not get his share (although his children would).

How to make a will

Drawing up a will is very straightforward these days, particularly with the help of computers and the Internet. A solicitor may charge you as little as £100 for a straightforward will and if you and your partner create identical wills (called mirror wills) you are likely to get a reduced rate for the two. A solicitor will usually store your will for you without charge.

However, a will can be perfectly valid without being drawn up or witnessed by a solicitor. It is possible to write your own will, perhaps with the aid of a will-writing kit, which you can buy from supermarkets, stationers or online. But only consider a DIY will if your affairs are straightforward. The DIY approach leaves you open to making a mistake, and if this should happen, there is nobody to blame but yourself. You could also go to a will writer, who is not a qualified lawyer but will still charge you for making a will. Make sure you check the firm's credentials thoroughly.

Older parents

One big issue for financial planning is that people are having children later in life. A few years back it would be usual for children to leave home and become financially independent while their parents are in their forties, or at least in their early fifties, but these days many parents in their forties still have young children, or even babies, at home.

If you are thinking of waiting to have children later on, this might be a good thing as you will probably be financially more secure and in a better paid job than you were in your early twenties. But it also means that just at the point where you start thinking about planning for retirement, you also have to think about savings and investing for your child or children.

The likelihood is that at some point you will face conflicting demands for your spare cash. Do you put it towards your retirement or help your kids to get a decent education? Even if you try to do both, you won't be able to save up for every event in your child's life. You will have to prioritise, possibly with the aid of an independent financial adviser who can help you see the big picture of your financial situation and weigh up the importance of your financial goals.

Most financial advisers agree that where you have to choose between educating your children privately and saving for retirement, you should opt to save for retirement.

There will be other difficult choices too. For example, you may have to choose between paying your child's university tuition fees or a deposit on their first home. A financial planner may point out that it can be better to let your child fund the university fees through low-cost student loans and for you to continue saving to build up a larger deposit. This is because a financial planner can project your child's financial situation years into the future and work out that he or she will save more money in the long term by having a smaller mortgage, as the interest rate on a typical mortgage is much higher than that on a student loan.

You will also need to make sure that you don't prioritise your child's financial future over your own. Mothers, in particular, tend to prioritise their kids. It's the natural instinct to want to provide every advantage and comfort for your children. But this can be a costly mistake if you sacrifice your own secure financial future for your children's non-essentials. And your children won't necessarily thank you for it, nor will they be happy to see their parents struggling to make ends meet in retirement.

But there are always ways to try and do both. Consider the cost of Christmas. It's estimated that at Christmas time, children receive almost £200-worth of presents on average. Is this really necessary? Around ten presents will be from people other than parents, but only six of these are likely to survive until March intact. So why not ask your family and friends to give your children something that will last much longer than three months – a savings top-up perhaps? Your children probably won't appreciate it now, but they may thank you in years to come.

According to investment company The Children's Mutual:

- family and friends spend an average of £180 per child at Christmas;
- children receive an average of 10 presents in addition to those given by their parents;
- 41 per cent of these presents will be broken by March; and
- collectively 46 million toys will be out of use by March.

7 Financial advice

Many people find that investing for their children is not something they can do on their own. At some point it is likely that you'll need to use the services of a financial adviser to help you with investment decisions. In fact, it is a good idea to visit a financial adviser when you first start to think about investing for children. But reading this book first will help you ascertain if your financial adviser is any good.

Although there are an estimated 18,000 financial advisers in the UK, finding quality advice is not straightforward. There are some very good financial advisers out there. The question is how to find one.

What is a financial adviser?
Financial adviser is a broad term that covers bank personnel, high street brokers, professional wealth managers and investment advisers.

What can a financial adviser do for me?
A financial adviser can recommend a savings product, a retirement plan, arrange a mortgage or insurance

policy, restructure your investments, give advice on the tax-efficiency of your portfolio or help with tax planning.

Most people seek straightforward advice on issues such as borrowing money, ensuring they have enough financial protection in place, and on how to start saving for the future. More knowledgeable financial consumers may be able to sort these 'basics' out themselves, but may need higher-level advice on, for example, investment and retirement planning issues.

You may think you can get along just fine making financial decisions and then you suddenly need the guiding hand of a professional – this is quite common, particularly if you want to send your child to private school, or as you near retirement.

What are the different types of financial adviser?

Getting the right type of financial advice is extremely important. Changes to the rules about financial advice mean there are currently three different types of adviser, which makes things a bit confusing.

■ **Tied advisers** can give advice on and recommend products from one company.

- **Multi-tied advisers** can give advice on and recommend products from a limited number of companies.
- **Independent financial advisers** can give advice on and recommend products from the whole market.

Each type of advice has its merits. However, if you have a large sum to invest or substantial family assets on which you need advice, you should find someone at the professional, top end of the market an independent financial adviser (IFA). In fact, some financial advisers require you to have a certain net worth before they will offer their services. If you are seeking advice on retirement planning, it's essential that you look for an independent financial adviser, who can recommend products from the whole of the market. Independent advice should be of higher quality and therefore to your considerable benefit longer term.

How do I find an independent financial adviser?

Most people first ask a trusted friend or relative for a recommendation. You could also ask your accountant or solicitor – they will know who are the best financial advisers in your local area. If neither of these options is available, use IFA Promotion's Find – an IFA service at www.unbiased. co.uk – to find an IFA close to your home. There are other contacts listed at the end of this chapter. It's best to interview and evaluate several financial advisers – at least three – to find the one that's right for you. The first session with an IFA is usually free of charge.

What qualifications are needed to practise as an IFA?

The minimum qualification that an IFA should have is the Certificate in Financial Planning, offered by the Chartered Insurance Institute. This is equivalent to an A-level. However, many areas of financial advice can be very complicated and demand a higher level of knowledge. More specialist professional qualifications – equivalent to a university degree – are on offer for complicated areas such as pensions, tax planning, trusts and specialist investment.

'Chartered Financial Planner' and the similar-sounding 'Certified Financial Planner' are high professional qualifications to look for. 'Chartered Financial Planner' is a title awarded by the Chartered Insurance Institute to experienced financial advisers who have a level of qualification equivalent to a first degree. The adviser must have worked in the industry for at least five years and have at least six Advanced Financial Planning Certificate level units, or the equivalent. Bear in mind that it is one thing being a technical genius, but an adviser has to be able to relate this to client's circumstances.

'Certified Financial Planner' is a similarly high-level qualification awarded by the Institute of Financial Planning but is more about the practical application of technical knowledge. It is a case study-based exam, which builds in report-based advice.

How do I pay for advice?

If an adviser has 'independent' status, he or she has to offer you the option of paying via fee. You can also pay by commission on the products sold or a mixture of fees and commission.

Anyone who has complicated advice needs should turn to the small but growing band of professional, fee-based advisers, who take no commission but get paid directly by the client for the ongoing advice they provide. A fee-based adviser is not necessarily the best, but is less likely to be biased than a commission-based one.

The big advantage of fees is that it makes it far more likely that the adviser will act with your best interests at heart. Fees mean there will be no conflict of interest and the adviser will not be tempted to recommend a product just because it pays him or her the biggest commission. IFAs may also offer you the option of offsetting commissions on products against the fee you would have paid. This is known as fee-based remuneration, which should also be a sign of quality.

Fees vary widely, depending on the quality of the adviser and location (advisers in Central London will be more expensive than those in the North of England). On average, fees are £150 an hour, or 1 per cent of your investment portfolio. This probably sounds expensive, but if you were to pay via commission on products sold, you might end up paying far more over time.

You also need to put the fees in context. Would you be happy to pay a plumber £60 an hour to sort out a problem in your bathroom? Surely it's worth paying £150 an hour to ensure your children's financial security and your own comfortable retirement?

Other points to consider

Remember that financial decisions can be sensitive and often give rise to strong emotions. Your financial adviser is a person to whom you will tell intimate details about your family and money, so you need to choose someone with whom you have good chemistry.

You need to trust your adviser and have confidence in his or her abilities. For this reason, the Financial Services Authority recommends you shop around for a financial adviser. There are contact organisations that can give you a list of advisers in your local area – see below. Even if friends and family recommend an adviser, talk to two or three before making your decision.

Before your first meeting with an adviser

If you want the best service from a financial adviser, you will have to do some background preparation before the first meeting. Knowing your financial priorities is essential. There is no point going to an IFA with the vague idea of a need for financial advice. You first need to have a firm idea of the life you wish to lead and your personal financial goals.

Identify the specific goals that you wish to save for. Examples include: buying a new car, a deposit on a home, a holiday of a lifetime, sending your children to university, paying off credit card debt, planning for retirement. Also, have a clear picture of the progress you have made towards obtaining each of these goals to date. Include how much you have saved, where your money is located and how much money you owe.

Next, you need to create an ideal timeframe. Ask yourself in an ideal world how soon you wish to accomplish these goals. Categorise each goal as to whether it is short-term (one year or less), medium-term (one to three years) or long-term (five or more years).

If you communicate all this to the adviser, you should get a better service.

Questions to ask an adviser

What experience do you have?

Find out how long he or she has been in practice and the different companies with which they have been associated.

What qualifications do you have?

Qualifications are not everything – experience is often just as valuable. However, higher qualifications show that the IFA has a certain level of knowledge. Find out what steps the adviser takes to stay on top of current changes and developments in the financial planning field.

What is your approach to financial planning?

Ask the adviser about the type of clients and financial situations he or she typically likes to work with. Some have a holistic approach to your finances, while others may specialise in advising on specific areas, for example mortgages, or in helping certain types of clients, for example doctors and dentists.

Will you be the only person working with me?

The adviser may work with you directly or may have others in the office, or outside the office, to assist. You may want to meet everyone who will be working with you. If the adviser works with professionals outside his or her own practice (such as lawyers or accountants) to carry out financial recommendations, get a list of their names to check on their backgrounds.

When and where will meetings take place?

Some advisers expect clients to go to the office during working hours for meetings. Others are more flexible, offering evening appointments and home visits. If it's hard to escape from your own workplace during the day, the option of evening or home meetings could be a valuable one.

Could you show me some references from satisfied clients?

Whether it's a financial adviser or a plumber, then personal recommendation is always a great start – but if you don't have that, it's good to be able to see that other clients have received sound advice.

What happens if you leave the firm or retire?

Your relationship with your financial adviser will be an ongoing one, renewed as your circumstances change. If your adviser is a one-man band approaching retirement, you will want to know who will step into his or her shoes. With larger firms, where staff turnover may be more of an issue, it's worth clarifying how client handovers are handled.

Be your own financial adviser

If you are confident and knowledgeable about money matters, you could manage your own financial affairs and investments while using the guiding hand of a professional in the instances where your own knowledge falls short.

Reading books like this one is a good start in building up your financial knowledge. There are also several financial magazines, and newspapers run regular money sections that keep you updated on the fast-moving financial sector. Plus, of course, there is a vast amount of information on the Internet.

Background reading on financial matters and doing your own investment research will help you identify the more professional advisers and monitor the quality of advice you receive.

Useful contacts

The online **Find an IFA** service at IFA Promotion (www.unbiased.co.uk; tel. 0800 085 3250) will provide the names and addresses of four independent financial advisers in your local area.

The **Institute of Financial Planning** (www. financialplanning.org.uk; tel. 0117 945 2470) has a national register of fee-based financial planners.

My Local Adviser (www.mylocaladviser.co.uk) enables you to identify and locate financial advisers in your area.

The **Personal Finance Society**'s Find an Adviser website (www.findanadviser.org) can help you find advisers in your local area who have passed at least three financial planning examinations.

The **Association of Private Client Investment Managers and Stockbrokers** (www.apcims.co.uk; tel. 020 7247 7080) provides a directory of its member stockbrokers and investment managers.

The **Association of Solicitor Investment Managers** (www.asim.org.uk; tel. 01732 783 548) provides a directory of solicitors who give legal and investment advice.

The **Financial Services Authority**'s consumer helpline (tel. 0845 606 1234) allows you to check that the firms you contact are authorised.

Basics of saving and investing

There is no perfect investment – otherwise we would all be rich. If you want your child's money to be safe, then you won't get a great return. But if you take some risk, the pot could double or triple overnight – or you could lose the lot by the morning. You have to balance risk and reward.

Learning how to invest is a daunting task for most people because it means you have to learn a bit about the stock market. But if you take the task seriously, a little knowledge can go a long way.

Investment strategy is inextricably linked to the goals for which you wish to use the money. These aims will dictate how you invest. Your child may need a small lump sum at certain times, for example school trips, or a large lump sum for other events, such as university fees or a wedding. Some goals will be near at hand – a school trip next spring, and others will be a long time ahead – a university education in 15 years' time.

Saving and investing for your children is something that you need to assess within your own financial goals. You should make sure that you are putting aside enough for retirement, for example, before committing extra funds to your children.

The difference between saving and investing

Saving and investing are both things that we do with our spare money, but there are key differences. Saving is a way of giving our day-to-day life some security so that we don't find ourselves short of cash in an emergency. Investing is more about planning for expensive events a few years in the future, like a child's first house or 20 years of retirement.

When you save money in a bank or building society account, you are guaranteed to get back the sum you put in, plus interest. Investing gives you no such guarantee. Your capital (the money you invest at the start) is at risk (you could lose the lot). In return for taking on this risk, you expect to get a much higher rate of return than that offered by the bank or building society account.

Unfortunately, inflation can make the return on cash accounts look miserable. If you are investing for the long term – more than five years – then experts agree that you should be putting your money in shares, also called equities.

Buying shares means investing in companies like British Airways, Shell, Marks & Spencer, Tesco, Vodafone, United

Utilitities and Unilever, plus other smaller companies that you may not have heard of.

After recent stock market turmoil, you may think that this is the last place you should be thinking of putting your money. Many investors saw their stock market investments halve in value in 2008. But if you have some courage, and a long-term perspective, this could actually be a very good time to put your money into the stock market.

Lots of studies have shown that over the years shares produce the best returns of all the different asset classes. One of the best known and most respected studies is the annual Barclays Capital Equity Gilt Study. The February 2008 Study showed that UK equities have made on average a real return of 7.2 per cent a year over the last 50 years. In contrast, cash has returned just 2 per cent a year.

Note that these figures show what shares have produced in the past and there is no guarantee that shares will continue to perform in this way. So you have to be comfortable with the worst case scenario, that you may lose your entire investment. Nevertheless, past performance, though no guarantee of future returns, is the only thing that investors really have to indicate roughly what their investments might return in future.

The year 2008 was terrible for equities, and the ten years to the end of 2008 were a 'lost decade' in which investors who prudently re-invested their dividends from equities have lost money after inflation. Over the last century and a bit there have been 16 ten-year periods like the past decade. But each one has been followed by a brilliant ten-year period for equities, on average producing annual returns of 10.8 per cent. So if you're starting investing now, this could well be the start of a period of growth in the stockmarket.

Shares will have good years and bad years, good months and bad months. This is why you have to invest for the long term, to smooth out the bumps in performance. You'll need to be in a position to put money aside in shares for at least five years, preferably a decade. And this must be money that you can afford to lose: in other words, that you – and your child – could survive without in your day-to-day lives.

If you are going to invest in shares yourself, without expert guidance, you'll have to dedicate lots of time and effort to successful stock picking. Most people don't have this sort of time and therefore prefer to invest in funds managed by professional fund managers. However, if you want to take the DIY approach to investing in shares, read some books about stock picking and investment strategies, and if you really want to get ahead in the stock market, becoming familiar with accounting is a necessity.

Power of compounding

To Albert Einstein, compound interest was the eighth wonder of the world. He is quoted as saying: 'The most powerful force in the universe is compound interest.'

When it comes to investing, compounding means that you earn interest on your initial investment, as well as on any other interest you may have accumulated. If you earn 5 per cent on £100, after a year you'll have £105. After two years, you'll have not £110, but £110.25. And, after 18 years, you'll have not £190 but £241.

Another important fact about compounding is that a small increase in the rate of return can produce a big impact over time. If you raise the rate of interest to 7 per cent on your £100, after 18 years you'll have £338. That's £97 more than if you'd had a 5 per cent return.

So if you are offered two investments that aim to yield 7 per cent, but one charges 1.5 per cent to manage the investment and the other charges 0.5 per cent, go for the cheapest. That 1 per cent difference in charges can make all the difference to the end result.

The benefits of saving early in your child's life – even if it is only small amounts – are greatly magnified by compounding. As time passes, the power of compounding accelerates dramatically. That £100 invested at 7 per cent gives a return of £7 in the first year, £13 in year ten, and £23 in year 18.

Getting started with investing as early as possible can make a big difference in how much wealth is ultimately accumulated. So don't delay, start today.

Table 1: Power of compounding over 18 years (£100 invested at 5 per cent interest)

Year 1	£105
Year 2	£110
Year 3	£115
Year 4	£121
Year 5	£127
Year 6	£134
Year 7	£140
Year 8	£147
Year 9	£155
Year 10	£162
Year 11	£171
Year 12	£179
Year 13	£188
Year 14	£197
Year 15	£207
Year 16	£218
Year 17	£229
Year 18	£241

Table 2: Power of compounding over 18 years (£100 invested at 7 per cent interest)

Year 1	£107
Year 2	£114
Year 3	£122
Year 4	£131
Year 5	£140
Year 6	£150
Year 7	£160
Year 8	£171
Year 9	£183
Year 10	£196
Year 11	£210
Year 12	£225
Year 13	£240
Year 14	£257
Year 15	£275
Year 16	£295
Year 17	£315
Year 18	£338

The Rule of 72

Doing compound interest problems in your head is tricky, but the Rule of 72 gives you a lightning fast method of determining how good (or not so good) a potential investment is likely to be. The Rule holds that in order to find the number of years required to double your money at a given interest rate, you can just divide the interest rate into 72.

For example, if you want to know how long it will take to double your money at 7 per cent interest, divide 7 into 72 and you'll get ten years. The rule of 72 is remarkably accurate, as long as the interest rate is less than 20 percent. You can also run it backwards. If you want to double your money in six years, just divide 6 into 72 to find that it will require an interest rate of about 12 per cent.

Lump sum or regular savings

Many investors invest lump sums, either at the end of the tax year (when they know how much extra they can save) or when they think they will benefit from stock market conditions.

Lump sums are not necessarily the best strategy, however, as the odds for getting market timing decisions right are terrible. A better option is to commit money to an investment plan on a regular and consistent basis. Regular savings plans remove the need to make market-timing decisions and also enable you to benefit from 'pound-cost averaging'. By investing the same amount each month, you are automatically buying more units or shares when prices are low and less when prices are high. Because you automatically buy more units when prices fall, the average cost of units you buy will be lower than the actual average price over the same period.

In a year when the market fluctuates around its starting point, ending up with very little increase, a regular savings plan could beat the same money invested as a lump sum at the start of the year. The more erratic the price performance of a fund, the greater the positive effects of pound-cost averaging.

The two enemies of investors: inflation and tax

If the time when your child will need the money is many years ahead, anything that is going to eat into your investment returns is a problem. That is why the two biggest enemies of investors are inflation and tax. Unfortunately, it is difficult to avoid the effects of inflation eroding your child's savings and investments. But there are plenty of things you can do to reduce the amount of tax you pay.

Inflation

Inflation is relatively low these days, but it can still have a powerful effect on your savings. This is why you should not put your money under the mattress. You have to make it grow.

Money languishing in bank accounts that pay less than 1 per cent interest is losing its value on a daily basis. That's fine, you say. I have my child's money in an account that pays 5 per cent, so I'm doing really well. Wrong! If you are a taxpayer, you are paying 20 per cent tax on that interest. So you are actually getting a return of 4 per cent on your money.

Let's say it has to earn at least 3 per cent to beat the annual increase in the cost of everyday living. The first 3 per cent of the return enables your money to hold its value. So you're only getting a 'real return' of 1 per cent. Now that headline rate of 5 per cent return doesn't seem so great. Over 10 years at 1 per cent, £100 invested would only grow to £110.46. Oh dear.

And with studies showing that many people feel actual inflation is far higher than the government's figures, the cost of living could be rising at a much faster pace than the government would have us believe. If this is true, then it becomes even more important never to forget about inflation and to consider investments that will beat this hidden enemy.

Tax

'In this world nothing is certain but death and taxes.' (*Benjamin Franklin.*)

Tax is inevitable and unavoidable. It's everywhere and affects everyone in countless ways; as individuals, employees and business owners. However, taxation is complicated and confusing and therefore widely misunderstood. Half of those surveyed by accountants PricewaterhouseCoopers believe that prescription charges and passport fees are taxes, when neither are.

Despite 31 million (70 per cent) of us claiming to resent rising tax bills, over three-quarters (78 per cent) of UK adults admit to doing nothing to help reduce the amount they pay, according to research from IFA Promotion.

An important key to getting your finances organised is to understand how tax reduces your income. From your income you're going to make savings. So if you can pay less tax, you can make greater savings for your children. I must emphasise here that I am concerned with legitimate ways to help reduce your tax bill – tax avoidance rather than tax evasion.

Be aware that your investments will be subject to tax. Putting your money into tax-efficient investments is a good idea because it will increase the amount you get back at the end of the investment period.

To tax experts, 1 June is known as Tax Freedom Day, and marks the theoretical point in the year at which we stop working for the government and start working for ourselves. The average British taxpayer spends the first 151 days of the year working to earn enough to pay off their tax burden to the government. So that's five months' work, to pay tax bills, and only seven months of the year earning money for ourselves.

It's disheartening to think that for nearly half of the year we are working simply to pay our tax bill, which is why it's so important that you make your hard-earned cash work for you. If you are willing to spend a few spare hours getting your finances in order, rather than paying unnecessary money in taxes, then you stand to reap substantial rewards in the long term.

There are many so-called 'tax-efficient' savings and investment products that can give your savings and investments a boost. However, there is a common saying among financial experts – 'don't let the tax tail wag the investment dog'. You mustn't invest in a product simply for its tax advantages. There are many bad 'tax-efficient' savings and investment products. For instance, if a product is going to pay a mediocre interest rate or give poor investment growth, then the tax advantage will be overridden by the money you lose compared to other better performing savings and investment products.

The reasons why you could be paying more tax than you need to are numerous, but with an understanding of the taxes most likely to affect your finances, and with some simple planning, you can cut your tax bill.

Income tax

Do you really understand how your income is taxed? If you fill out a self-assessment form you're more likely to be aware. However, if you're paid through PAYE (Pay As You Earn), you may not have given it a thought until now.

In the tax year 2009/10, the first £6,475 of your earned income is free of tax. The next slice is taxed at the basic rate of 20 per cent. Earnings over a certain amount – £43,875 in 2009/10 – are taxed at 40 per cent. Being a higher rate taxpayer has all sorts of implications for saving and investing.

You can pay less tax by making the best use of your tax-free personal allowances. This is particularly relevant if you are married and you and your spouse pay different rates of tax. If, for example, one of you is a higher-rate taxpayer and the other a basic-rate or non-taxpayer, you can cut your tax liability in half by transferring income-yielding assets like building society deposits or shares to the lower earner.

National Insurance

This is not technically a tax, but it still reduces your income so I'm including it in this section.

It is possible to reduce National Insurance contributions using 'salary sacrifice', an arrangement between an employer and employee where the employee agrees to a reduction in salary or bonus in exchange for a non-cash benefit provided by the employer. For example, this benefit can be a payment to the employee's pension scheme. And crucially, by reducing the salary or bonus, both employee and employer save on NI.

The employee benefits, as a higher level of pension payment can be made without reducing take-home pay. As an alternative, the original level of pension payment can be made and the employee will have an increase in take-home pay. And the employer benefits because they will pay reduced NI. However, the employer does have the option to pay all or some of the NI saving into the employee's pension arrangement.

Bear in mind that, with either option, salary is being genuinely sacrificed and, therefore, any outgoings that are based on salary may be affected, for example a mortgage or credit card. In addition, some state benefits are linked to earnings, so these may be affected too.

Capital gains tax

This is the other big tax that affects investors. You have capital gains if you invest money, it grows and then you cash it in for a profit. The profit is potentially liable to tax.

All individuals have an annual exemption for capital gains tax (CGT) which, in the 2008/09 tax year, was £9,600. So any gains up to this amount within a tax year are free of tax. You should use this allowance efficiently, perhaps by transferring assets between spouses to make the most of both of your CGT allowances – IFA Promotion estimates that £510 million could be saved in this way.

Inheritance tax

The second most-hated tax after council tax is inheritance tax. This used to be something that only concerned the very wealthy, but the massive rise in house prices over the past ten years means many people, particularly those in the South East, are now affected.

Tax credits

Find out if you are eligible for tax credits and claim them: £2.3 billion of 'free money' is up for grabs from HMRC and the Department for Work and Pensions in the form of Pension Credits, Child Tax Credits and Working Family Tax Credit. Visit www.hmrc.gov.uk/TAXCREDITS for more information.

Your tax return

There is no reason to feel inadequate because, despite being an intelligent person, you feel slightly sick at the thought of preparing your tax return. The tax rules are so complicated that many accountants would struggle to calculate their own tax without software to help them.

However, the Self Assessment tax return form is an annual chore that comes around with alarming regularity. There is no avoiding the job, so you'd better get on with it and meet the deadline to avoid the £100 fine for late submission.

If you want HMRC to calculate your tax bill, you have to send in your tax return by 31 October. After that date, they will still calculate your tax, but do not guarantee to get the calculation to you before the payment date, which is 31 January.

Another reason for getting your tax return in before the end of October is that you can request that any tax underpayments below £2,000 can be collected via your PAYE tax code.

Make sure you sort out your Self Assessment form within the deadlines – £463 million tax waste could be wiped out if all forms arrived present and correct by the 31 January deadline. Self Assessment forms received after the deadline incur penalties of £100; further penalties and errors make up the balance of tax wasted in this way.

Also make sure you fill out the form correctly. There are two mistakes that automatically result in the return being rejected. The first is that you enter a tick to confirm that you have a particular source of income, but the relevant supplementary sheets are not included with the return, so it becomes incomplete. Get on the telephone to the Self Assessment orderline on 0845 9000 404 to request any missing supplementary sheets. But the most common reason for the rejection of a tax return is that it is not signed. So, after checking your return is complete and accurate, make sure you sign and date it before putting it in the post.

Visit www.unbiased.co.uk/personal-finance/tax/ for tips on how to become more tax-efficient, plus a useful calculator to help you work out how much tax you are wasting each year.

Tax implications of investing for children

For parents who invest on behalf of their children, there may be tax consequences. For children under 18, interest above £100 paid on a child's deposits or investments set up in the name of a parent is treated as the income of the parent and the whole sum is taxable (not just the excess over £100 a year). This means that an investment may incur a tax charge even when the intended beneficiaries are not taxpayers. So it pays to find tax-efficient investments such as the Child Trust Fund when you are investing on behalf of a child.

Children, like adults, can receive a certain amount of income tax free. This is called the Personal Allowance and is set each year – for the tax year 2008/09, it was £6,035. As long as a child's annual income (including interest) is below this amount, the child will be able to receive interest without having the tax deducted and/or claim back any tax they shouldn't have paid.

Make sure you fill out a special form, R85, to ensure that your children don't pay tax on any accounts you open on their behalf. (Parents or guardians need to fill in a separate form for each account.) To claim back tax for a child, parents or guardians make a separate claim to HMRC, using Form R40.

A child can't claim to receive savings interest tax free if his or her income is above the Personal Allowance. But they will be able to reclaim some tax if they have not used the starting rate (10 per cent) limit for savings only (up to £2,320 above the Personal Allowance).

You can download Forms R85 and R40 at www. direct.gov.uk.

Giving money to your children or investing on their behalf

You can give to a child or invest on their behalf as much money as you like. But if you're a parent or step-parent and the money you give your child earns more than £100 interest a year, this interest will be taxed as if it were your own.

The £100 limit only applies to parents and step-parents. Grandparents and other adults who give money to children are not liable to pay the tax if the interest exceeds £100 a year.

If an account earns 4 per cent interest, then it would have to hold more than £2,500 to breach this £100 rule. The income tax is not debited directly from the account and the onus is on parents to make arrangements to pay this as part of their own personal tax liability.

Note that the £100 income rule applies separately to each parent, so if a parent wishes to save a £1,000 per year for a child, then it would be more tax efficient for each parent to make separate gifts.

When a child turns 16

Once children reach the age of 16, they are responsible for the tax on their interest payments, so they'll need to fill in their own Form R85 (provided their income stays below the Personal Allowance). Therefore, accounts held in someone else's name should be transferred to them – otherwise the bank or building society will immediately have to start to deduct tax from the interest (it may be possible to reclaim this tax, as described earlier).

How safe is your money?

In 2008 many people got very worried about the safety of their savings and investments. Not only did the stock market plummet, but the previously unthinkable happened and banks went bust.

Northern Rock was the first victim of the credit crunch. Because of the global financial crisis in summer 2007, Northern Rock found it difficult to borrow the cash to run its day-to-day operations. When it became public knowledge that the bank was in trouble, customers queued to get their money out. The bank was taken into public ownership in February 2008.

Customers of the online bank Icesave, which went bust in October 2008, spent a couple of sleepless nights worrying that they wouldn't see their money again, before the UK government decided that it would guarantee them full compensation.

Always bear in mind that banks and financial institutions can go bust, and plan your savings and investments accordingly.

At the time of writing, two institutions were government owned and therefore completely safe homes for your money. These were Northern Rock, which, as mentioned above, was taken over by the government in February 2008, and National Savings and Investments, the government-backed savings bank. For more on National Savings and Investments products, turn to Chapter 11.

UK savers and investors have an important safety net in the form of the Financial Services Compensation Scheme (FSCS). But there are limits on what this will pay out in the event of a bank or other financial institution going bust.

The FSCS is the UK's statutory fund of last resort for customers of authorised financial services firms. It is very important to check that any organisation you are considering as a home for your money is authorised by the Financial Services Authority (FSA) to do business.

FSA authorisation means that the FSCS can pay compensation if a firm is unable, or likely to be unable, to pay claims made against it. Customers of unauthorised firms are not eligible for compensation. The FSCS is an independent body, set up under the Financial Services and Markets Act 2000 (FSMA) and its service is free to consumers. The FSCS protects:

- deposits;
- life and general insurance firms;
- investment business (on or after 28 August 1988);

- home finance (e.g. mortgage) advice and arranging (on or after 31 October 2004); and
- general insurance policies advice and arranging (on or after 14 January 2005).

The maximum levels of compensation

Deposits: £50,000 per person (for claims against firms declared in default from 7 October 2008).

100 per cent of the first £50,000.*

Investments: £48,000 per person.

100 per cent of the first £30,000 and 90 per cent of the next £20,000.

* The FSA changed the rules that govern compensation payments on 3 October 2008 to increase the total limit to £50,000. The limit came into effect on 7 October 2008. For deposit claims against firms declared in default between 1 October 2007 and 6 October 2008, the maximum level of compensation is £35,000 (100 per cent of £35,000). For deposit claims against firms declared in default before 1 October 2007, the maximum level of compensation is £31,700 (100 per cent of the first £2,000 and 90 per cent of the next £33,000).

Depositors may still receive a share of their savings above £50,000 back following any distribution of assets as part of the insolvency process for a failed bank. This would be a matter for the insolvency practitioner to determine and any recovery would, by necessity, vary according to the circumstances of the specific failure.

The actual level of compensation you receive will depend on the basis of your claim. The FSCS only pays compensation for financial loss.

Compensation limits are per person (per firm and type of claim).

Slightly different limits and rules apply if you have a claim against an insurer or a bank that was insolvent before the FSCS became operational (1 December 2001), or if your claim is against an investment firm that was declared in default before the FSCS became operational.

Home finance (e.g. mortgage) advice and arranging:
£48,000 per person (for business conducted on or after 31 October 2004).
100 per cent of the first £30,000 and 90 per cent of the next £20,000.

Long-term insurance (e.g. pensions and life assurance):
unlimited.
100 per cent of the first £2,000 plus 90 per cent of the remainder of the claim.

General insurance: unlimited.
Compulsory insurance (e.g. third party motor): 100 per cent of the claim. Non-compulsory insurance (e.g. home and general): 100 per cent of the first £2,000 plus 90 per cent of the remainder of the claim.

General insurance advice and arranging: unlimited (for business conducted on or after 14 January 2005).
100 per cent of the first £2,000 plus 90 per cent of the remainder of the claim. Compulsory insurance is protected in full.

For further information, visit www.fscs.org.uk or call 020 7892 7300.

So what do these compensation limits mean for your savings and investments? The most important thing to remember is not to put more than £50,000 with any banking organisation. It is also wise to spread your investments around between different investment firms.

Children's savings accounts

Holding money for your child in a cash deposit account is popular because it is easy to understand and safe. You know that you can get your money back, plus a little bit of interest on top. And it is highly unlikely that you'll lose your money, as history tells us that banks *rarely* go bust. The fact that they *can* go bust has painfully come to our attention in recent years. But there are government safeguards in place to protect your money – for more on this, see Chapter 9.

Cash should always be part of an investment portfolio, and if you are saving for the short term – less than five years – then it will be the main component. With interest rates hitting the lowest levels for 50 years in 2008, you're not going to get a great return on your capital. But neither will you lose your savings, as you might in the stock market.

If you have any children or grandchildren you may want to open a savings account for them to encourage them to save from an early age. Many banks and building societies offer special savings accounts for children and, generally, these work like adults' accounts, but often paying higher rates of interest.

There is no minimum age for a child's account to be opened. However most providers require a parent or guardian to open and run the account until the child is between 7 and 11 years old. Most children's accounts have to be closed by the time the child is 18, while a few can be kept open until the child is 24. Many come with incentives such as gift vouchers, but it makes more sense to go for an account paying a high interest rate rather than one with a low rate plus free gifts.

Most children's savings accounts are easy access, allowing money to be withdrawn without notice or penalty, but some accounts require notice to be given to allow a penalty-free withdrawal. The latter normally offer a higher level of interest than easy access accounts. Bond or term accounts offer the highest interest, but to receive this, the money invested normally has to be left in the account for a specific period. This could vary from one to five years, or some providers require money to be left until the child has reached a certain age.

It is a good idea to choose a children's account that is simple and has no strings attached, such as limits on your withdrawals, or interest rates which are made to look artificially high by the addition of an annual bonus that you could lose in some circumstances.

The trouble with bank and building society savings

accounts is that the interest earned is taxable. Most adult bank and building society accounts have 20 per cent tax deducted on the interest before it's paid. If you are a higher rate taxpayer you pay extra tax on the income from your savings through your self-assessment tax return.

Children are allowed a certain tax-free allowance (see p. 81). Parents or guardians need to fill in a separate form for each account.

National Savings and Investments

National Savings and Investments (NS&I) is a government-backed savings bank that offers cast-iron safety because it will never go bust. It has millions of customers and, in the aftermath of the credit crunch and several banks going bust, it has become more popular for its ultimate safe haven status. The price of safety is that the rates of return on many of its products can be lower than you might find elsewhere. However, it has several very useful and unique products that are tax free and cannot be found elsewhere.

One interesting option is the five-year **Children's Bonus Bonds**, which pay a guaranteed rate, free of tax. Children's Bonus Bonds are available in issues and each has its own rate of return – which you should check before you invest. You can invest a lump sum of as little as £25 up to £3,000 per issue.

National Savings and Investments adds interest each year, along with a bonus every five years until the child's 21st birthday, all tax free. You can invest in as many issues as you like, up to £3,000 per issue for each child. Unfortunately, at the time of writing, the rates weren't particularly good so you should check how they compare with the rates available from other savings accounts with banks and building societies.

The NS&I bank also offers **Premium Bonds**, where you have the chance to win tax-free prizes. There is a prize draw every month with two £1 million jackpots plus more than a million other tax-free prizes. The more bonds you have, the better your chances of winning. Anyone aged 16 or over can buy Premium Bonds and they can also be bought on behalf of under-16s by parents and grandparents.

The chances of winning a big prize with Premium Bonds are slim. The prize rate, albeit tax free, is lower than the rate paid on many savings accounts. The odds of winning the top £1 million prize are very slim – you have a greater chance of winning the Lottery jackpot. However, at the time of writing, when the Bank of England base rate was at a historic low of 1 per cent, the Premium Bond prize fund rate was 1.8 per cent – not fantastic but a lot better than some bank accounts. Although you won't lose your money if you don't win prizes, you may lose out to inflation. But if you want a bit of fun and a flutter, there is no harm in taking out the minimum £100 bond for a child, in addition to other investments.

Arguably the jewel in the crown of National Savings and Investments it its **Index-linked Savings Certificates**. These offer inflation-beating savings with tax-free returns.

With Index-linked Savings Certificates, the value of your investment increases in line with inflation as measured by the Retail Prices Index (RPI) and earns guaranteed interest rates on top – with all your returns tax free (which means that all returns are free of UK income tax and Capital Gains Tax). So you can be sure to keep ahead of rising prices.

The RPI measures the average change in the prices of goods and services bought by most households in the UK. It is compiled and published monthly by the Office for National Statistics (ONS).

You may have heard of another measure of inflation called the Consumer Prices Index, or CPI. The government now uses the CPI for its inflation target, although the RPI is still used, for example, for index-linking of pensions.

WHAT'S THE DIFFERENCE BETWEEN RPI AND CPI?

The RPI includes housing costs and council tax and is calculated in a different way, so it tends to be higher than the CPI. NS&I has always used the RPI to calculate increases in the value of Index-linked Savings Certificates and continues to do so. Both the RPI and CPI can go up or down and the difference between them can change. To check the latest official figures and find out more about how inflation is calculated, visit www.statistics.gov.uk.

Because inflation fluctuates, you won't know exactly how much you are going to receive until your certificates mature. But you can be sure that your money will have more spending power.

At the time of writing, inflation was easing off but many experts think it could take off with a vengeance in years to come as governments need to pay off debts (allowing inflation to rise is a great way of reducing a country's debt burden). So these are definitely investments to consider.

NS&I also offers an **Investment Account**, a straightforward passbook savings account with easy access to your money. Anyone aged seven or over can invest in this, and it can also be opened on behalf of under-sevens. Access to your money is at a UK Post Office branch or via post. The minimum deposit is £20. The rates are not good compared to other children's savings accounts; the main selling point is ultimate security.

For further information on all of these products, visit www.nsandi.com or call 0500 500 000.

12 Child Trust Funds

'A Child Trust Fund – established for each child at birth, endowed during their childhood years and available at age 18 – to which Britain as a nation contributes – expresses our shared belief that in our country every child should have the best possible start in life. . . . At age 18, on the basis of historic rates of return, the Child Trust Fund will accumulate assets that will enable all young people to have more of the choices that were once available only to some.'

So said Gordon Brown in his budget speech in 2003 when, as Chancellor of the Exchequer, he launched the Child Trust Fund (CTF).

It's hard not to like Child Trust Funds. After all, it's not often that the government doles out free money. Every child born since 1 September 2002 has a voucher worth at least £250 from the government to start a Child Trust Fund account.

It's important to consider a Child Trust Fund in any plans to invest for a child. But parents often find it difficult to decide what to do with the money. The government leaves the decision to you. And there are a host of Child Trust Fund providers lining up to take your money. Choice is good, but it can be confusing.

How CTFs work

At the birth of a child, a CTF is kick-started for them with an endowment of £250 from the government. At age seven, the child receives a top-up endowment of £250. Children from low-income families receive extra payments.

With a CTF, parents can choose the type of account the money is invested in, but when the child turns 16 he or she can have a say in how the money is invested. You can move the account to a different provider or change the type of account at any time.

Parents, other family members and friends can contribute a maximum of £1,200 a year to the fund. The money grows tax free until the child is 18, when he or she can spend it as they wish. If the full amount of £1,200 a year is contributed, the child may have a substantial nest egg at age 18.

The Children's Mutual, a provider of Child Trust Funds, has created an online calculator to help parents of young children work out how much they may need to save for the future: www.thechildrensmutual.co.uk/ctfcalculator. For example, if the £250 Child Trust Fund government voucher given to each child registered for Child Benefit (with another £250 from government due at age seven) were invested and a regular monthly contribution of £20 added, the account could pay out over £8,300 when the child turned 18. If this were increased to the maximum monthly contribution of £100, the potential payout could rise to a very healthy £37,100.

The key to maximising the potential of the CTF is to add to the account regularly. Currently, customers with The Children's Mutual pay an average of £24 a month into their children's CTFs. If kept up throughout the life of the CTF, this could give a child a lump sum of up to £9,750 when they reach age 18.

How much might a Child Trust Fund be worth at age 18?

£250 contribution at birth and age 7	£1,188
£250 contribution at birth and age 7, plus £1,200 a year	£40,500

Source: Bestinvest
Note: The illustrations assume an annual return of 6 per cent a year net of charges.

Choosing the right investment

Your Child Trust Fund decision can be seen as a microcosm for all your saving and investing decisions. If you understand all the options within the Child Trust Fund, then you will be pretty well set up to invest for your child and for yourself for the rest of your life.

There are three main types of CTF account:

- **savings accounts**, which invest in cash;
- **stakeholder accounts**, which invest in shares but have features to reduce the risk; and
- **share accounts**, which are higher risk.

Savings accounts

Savings accounts may look like the best bet. You may worry about losing your child's money and feel that the government vouchers will be safe in a savings account. However, over time, although your money would earn interest, it might not grow as much as it would if it was invested in shares, which would reduce your chances of turning it into a meaningful amount. You may also find that you struggle to beat inflation. The effect of inflation means that money in the account could lose value over the long term. This is because prices usually rise each year and so £250 won't buy you as much today as it did ten years ago.

Stakeholder accounts

The stakeholder concept was designed by the government for the CTF and recognises that shares are the best bet for long-term savings. If you don't make a decision to invest the government's vouchers in a particular CTF, after a certain period of time, the government will invest it in a stakeholder account.

Importantly, a stakeholder CTF has safeguards, including low charges and a switch to less risky investments from the child's 13th birthday. Once your child reaches 13, money in the account starts to be moved to lower-risk investments or assets, such as cash. Your CTF provider will consider how well shares are performing when deciding how much to move over into safer assets and how quickly. Basically, this kind of account protects against stock markets crashing just before the child reaches 18. For example, with a stakeholder account, if your child had turned 18 in 2009, he or she would have been mostly shielded from the crash of 2008, when the UK stock market suffered its worst year in history.

Stakeholder accounts have rules about how much you can contribute and how much you are charged. Once the account is open, all stakeholder providers must accept minimum contributions of £10 into a stakeholder account, but they can accept less if they wish. This will be an advantage if you only have small sums to invest.

The charge on the stakeholder account is limited to a maximum of 1.5 per cent a year. This means the charge can be no more than £1.50 for every £100 in the account. Although 1.5 per cent is by no means cheap – it is the average that most mainstream funds charge – charges on all other types of Child Trust Fund accounts are not limited in this way. So watch out for high charges on CTFs, as they can eat significantly into investment returns over time.

Many providers justify higher charges by citing high administration costs for handling small amounts of money – £10 is a small sum for an investment manager to administer. When you are investing in mainstream investment funds outside the CTF, the minimum contribution is often £500 or £1,000.

Share accounts

Share accounts invest your child's money by buying shares in companies. When those companies do well and the shares go up in value, they make money. But if the companies don't do well, then the shares may fall in value and you could lose money.

This type of account has the potential to do well when money is invested for a long time (18 years qualifies as a long time in the investment world). This is because poor performance of shares in some years can be made up for by good performance in others and, over a long time period, the stock market's value tends to rise more than it falls.

Investing in shares is more risky than putting money in a savings account as shares can lose value if companies are not performing well. But, in the past, an amount of money left for a long time in this type of account has grown more than the same amount left in a savings account. This is true for every 18-year period in the last 40 years.

However, nobody can promise that shares will continue to be the best long-term investment, so it's important to remember that shares can go down as well as up and that past performance is not a guarantee of how shares will perform in the future.

Topping up a CTF

If your family can afford to make contributions to a CTF in addition to the government vouchers, it is arguable whether a CTF is the best place for these funds. One big potential problem with the Child Trust Fund is that the account belongs to the child. Many parents do not like the idea of young Olivia or Jack having full control of the money at 18 and blowing the lot on partying or on a designer wardrobe. So if you are topping up a CTF, you must be aware that you have no control over how that money will be spent. You could, in effect, be giving a child a large sum of money at 18 only to see them squander it.

Unless you are absolutely confident that your child will be guided by your wishes in spending the CTF, the only way to guarantee that the money is spent, say, on university tuition fees, you will need to invest it outside a CTF, for example in an individual savings account (ISA), described in Chapter 13, or another form of investment for children.

Another problem is that the fund can't be accessed until the child turns 18. If you think you might need the money you contribute for private school fees when the child is 12, or for a school trip at 15, the CTF won't be suitable.

Some experts argue that there can be better choice and better value outside the CTF regime for top-up investments. The range of investments available within CTFs is at present limited. For example, few of the big City fund managers opted to offer Child Trust Funds – they felt it was simply not worth their while. Fidelity is a notable exception to the list of CTF providers – the UK's largest retail fund manager's decision not to offer CTFs was seen as a snub to the government.

In terms of value, charges on Child Trust Funds are often very high compared to other funds because, firstly, the government allows the stakeholder providers to charge 1.5 per cent; secondly, providers have little incentive to charge less and, thirdly, providers argue that administration costs are high because they have to deal with amounts as little as £10 a month.

Child Trust Fund providers

You can see a full list of Child Trust Fund providers on the official CTF website at www.childtrustfund.gov.uk.

Friendly societies

Some providers of Child Trust Funds are friendly societies that offer their own fund range – for example **Family Investments** (www.familyinvestments.co.uk), which has two equity funds, or those which have links with external fund managers to provide the investment funds – for example, **The Children's Mutual** (www.thechildrensmutual.co.uk), which offers a choice of 11 funds from four leading fund managers.

City fund managers

There are only two City fund managers that offer Child Trust Funds. These are as follows.

F&C Asset Management (www.fandc.co.uk): The F&C Child Trust Fund gives you a range of 16 investment trusts to choose from plus a stakeholder account that invests in the F&C FTSE All-Share Tracker Fund. Among the fund manager's range of investment trusts, the most popular choice for children's savings is the group's flagship global growth trust, Foreign & Colonial. This trust is the oldest collective investment fund in the UK. It invests in more than 700 companies in 35 countries, so you are really getting a huge spread of investments for your money. F&C says Foreign & Colonial Investment Trust is its most popular CTF option. The total expenses are just 0.53 per cent, making it almost certainly the lowest-cost managed fund option within any CTF, being just under a third of the cost of most stakeholder CTFs and half those of F&C's FTSE All-Share Tracker Fund stakeholder options. The investment is also much better diversified.

The F&C FTSE All-Share Tracker Fund, in which my daughter's CTF fund was invested at the time of writing, is a low-cost stakeholder option on the market; other providers typically offer tracker funds at 1.5 per cent, a third more. The fund has a Total Expense Ratio of 0.39, but on top of this adds an annual CTF charge of 0.7 per cent to cover the costs of the plan's third-party administrator. So even though I have the cheapest tracker option for the CTF, I'm still being charged 1.09 per cent a year for a tracker fund, much more than many tracker funds outside a CTF that charge less than 0.5 per cent a year.

Jump CTF (www.jumpsavings.co.uk): Jump Child Trust Fund is based on Witan Investment Trust, a leading global investment fund that invests in hundreds of blue-chip stocks and shares, spread across the world's markets to minimise risk. All CTF providers must offer a stakeholder option and, for this purpose, Jump offers the Halifax FTSE 100 Index Tracking fund, though the company hopes that most people will choose Witan. One advantage of Witan over the tracker fund is that it has a very low expense ratio – only 0.46 per cent, compared with 1.5 per cent for the tracker.

Self-select accounts

To get the fullest range of investments, you should opt for a self-select Child Trust Fund, offered by a handful of stockbrokers. This will allow you access to all unit trust and investment trusts, plus direct share dealing. You make the investment decisions. However, a self-select CTF is potentially more expensive than a unit trust or investment trust as you have to pay an annual plan charge.

Ethical investment options

You can invest ethically by using the self-selection option outlined above. Otherwise, ethical options include the following.

The Children's Mutual offers the Evergreen fund from fund management group Insight. This fund aims to combine long-term growth with investing ethically. It invests in companies throughout the world whose products, processes or services contribute to the restoration and renewal of the earth's ecology or to a cleaner and healthier environment.

Family Investments offers a stakeholder CTF that invests in an ethical fund. The fund avoids investing your child's money in any companies that generate significant turnover from: alcohol or tobacco; export of goods or services for military users; supplying ozone-depleting chemicals; testing of cosmetics or toiletries on animals; using intensive farming methods; extracting or importing tropical hardwood; trade in prohibited pesticides; activities which significantly pollute waterways. It also avoids company groups that have registered companies in a significant number of countries identified as violating human rights.

Individual savings accounts

If you are not already using your annual individual savings account (ISA) allowance, you could use an ISA to save for children. For many parents, topping up an ISA is a better option than a Child Trust Fund (see Chapter 12) as it gives greater flexibility and choice. There are the same income tax and capital gains tax benefits but, with an ISA, there are no government rules dictating who your investment should benefit and when they should have access to it.

A potential problem with using an ISA to save for a child is that there is no line drawn between your own pot of money and that of the child. There is, therefore, the temptation to dip into the money for your own needs. It is also highly likely that you may be already using your ISA allowance for your own long-term savings – to build up a retirement fund, for example.

ISAs are a straightforward tax-efficient financial planning tool that can be used to plan for your future, whatever your age, because they can be used to achieve short- and long-term savings goals. For short-term goals, you can use cash ISAs and for long-term goals, stocks and shares ISAs.

The tax advantages of ISAs can help turn your pennies into pounds. Savers could earn a massive £73,611 extra over a lifetime if their cash savings were invested in a tax-efficient ISA, rather than an ordinary bank account – and the extra savings figure would double for high-rate taxpayers, according to research from Alliance & Leicester Savings. So if your hard-earned cash is languishing in an ordinary bank or building society account, start moving it into an ISA straight away.

The great thing about ISAs is they allow you to save money for the short or long term, but you aren't locked into a particular timescale. If you change your mind along the way, you can cash in your ISA and spend the money on something different.

If you are using an ISA to save for your retirement at 65, but then, when you are 50, a family emergency crops up that needs a large sum of money, you can dip into your ISA. This flexibility is why ISAs are so popular. The downside is that you have to be very disciplined about the money you have in your ISA and resist the temptation to dip into it for non-essential spending money.

History of ISAs

ISAs were launched by the Labour government in 1999 to encourage people to save for their future. They replaced the popular personal equity plans (PEPs) introduced by the Conservatives and which had proved a great success – more than one in three adults owned a PEP. Many continue to own PEPs, but they have now morphed into ISAs. If you started investing before 1999, you may have some of the old-style PEPs. All PEP accounts automatically became stocks and shares ISAs on 6 April 2008 and became subject to ISA rules. PEP holders can still use their full annual ISA allowances.

The attraction of ISAs is that any money accrued within them is free of both income tax and capital gains tax. ISAs are held by more than 16 million individual investors, with total policies worth more than £180 billion.

When ISAs were introduced in 1999, the government initially said that the scheme would only run until 2009. Thankfully, the government has now changed its stance and guaranteed that the existing annual ISA allowances will continue indefinitely. The original £7,000 limit on annual savings has been extended. This is very good news for investors.

ISA basics

You can invest up to £7,200 each year in an ISA. Each tax year ends on 5 April and this is the cut-off point for investing. While you can put money in and take money out of an ISA during the year, you cannot put in more than £7,200.

For example, if you put in £3,000 in May, and then withdrew £1,000 for a family emergency in June, you would be left with £2,000 in your ISA. However, if your great aunt were then to leave you a £5,000 inheritance in September, you could not put the whole of that sum into the ISA – only £4,200.

Anyone over 16 may invest in a cash ISA, but you have to be over 18 to invest in a stocks and shares ISA. You don't have to be employed or to be a taxpayer to take out an ISA.

Eligible ISA investments include: cash deposits (including National Savings and Investments products); and stocks and shares, including unit trusts, open-ended investment companies (Oeics) and investment trusts.

New ISA rules

Higher limits for annual investment in ISAs came into force on 6 April 2008. Each year you can save up to £3,600 in a cash ISA and up to £7,200 in a stocks and shares ISA, within an overall annual limit for new investment of £7,200.

People with cash ISAs from previous years can transfer the money into a stocks and shares ISA. Savers who choose to make the switch can still invest the maximum £7,200 a year in their ISA that tax year in addition to the money they have switched. This flexibility can be useful. It is not, however, possible to transfer funds in the other direction, i.e. from a shares ISA to a cash ISA.

The changes mean some savers have a lower investment ceiling for their stocks and shares than previously. The new, raised cash limit of £3,600 means that someone who chooses to save the maximum cash each year will only be able to invest £3,600 in stocks and shares – less than the previous limit of £4,000 a year.

How to use ISAs in your financial plans

Ideally, put enough in cash ISAs to act as an emergency fund. If you have an investment goal that is less than five years from now, use cash ISAs to build up funds. For any financial goal that is more than five years away, you can build up funds in stocks and shares ISAs. This might be your retirement fund. Or it might be a fund to put your kids through university. Or a fund to buy a new car, or pay for a round the world trip. Or just for a rainy day.

Something to think about

If ISAs do survive – and if there is a change of government, they may not – you could, over the next 18 years, put away £129,600 (18 × £7,200). If this simply grows enough to beat inflation and hold its value, by the time your child goes to university, the total sum invested could generate a tax-free annual income of £6,480, assuming that interest rates at the time are 5 per cent. Even if you could only generate an income of 3 per cent, you would have £3,888 a year to help your child through university. The capital could be kept as your retirement fund, or you could dip into it to offer your child further help.

If your ISA were to grow above the rate of inflation, the pot would be much larger and your child's university days would be much more comfortable. You would expect your ISA to grow much more than inflation if it were invested in the stock market. So simply putting money into ISAs over 18 years could get your child the result you desire.

Cash ISAs

You buy a cash ISA, which is essentially a cash savings account with tax advantages, from most banks and building societies. Many cash ISAs can be opened with as little as £1, and the balance is available to be withdrawn at any time, so there is really no excuse for not having one. If you want to build up a cash fund for emergencies, it makes sense to do this using a cash ISA as you won't pay savings tax on the money held inside.

If you pay tax at the basic rate, you will usually pay 20 per cent tax on your savings interest, but interest earned within a cash ISA is tax free. For example, if you invested £3,000 in a cash ISA and the account paid interest at 5 per cent, you'd earn £30 more in a year than you would if you invested that money in an ordinary bank or building society earning the same 5 per cent interest rate.

In the ordinary account, the 5 per cent interest rate would become 4 per cent after 20 per cent savings tax, so instead of earning £150 in interest, you would earn just £120.

If interest rates were higher, say 6 per cent, then you would earn £36 more in a year in the cash ISA (£180 interest, compared with £144 interest in the ordinary taxed account).

Stocks and shares ISAs

If your goal is to build up a pot of money that you can use to help your child pay off their student debt in ten years' time or put down as a deposit on a house in 20 years' time, you are a 'growth' investor. ISAs are ideal for growth investors because any capital gains generated within the ISA wrapper are tax free. Growth traditionally comes from stock market investments, also called equities. You can put up to £7,200 in equities each year, either directly (in a self-select ISA) or via a collective fund, in which your

113

investments are pooled with those of other investors and managed by a professional fund manager.

Most stocks and shares ISA investors choose collective funds such as unit trusts and investment trusts.

Self-select ISAs

Sophisticated active investors who want flexibility in their ISA holdings may be interested in a self-select ISA. Usually provided and administered by stockbrokers, self-select ISAs are designed for mixing and matching funds, equities, gilts, bonds and cash. You make your own investment decisions, picking stocks such as Tesco or Vodafone to hold in your ISA.

Self-select ISAs run by stockbrokers are for active investors who want flexibility in their ISA holding, plus the ability to trade within their ISA wrapper. A self-select ISA can hold individual equities, investment trusts, gilts, bonds and cash as well as (or instead of) unit trusts and Oeics.

Stockbrokers usually charge either a flat fee for the ISA wrapper or a percentage charge of the portfolio value. On top of that there will be dealing costs.

Self-select ISAs vary not only in the charges levied, but also in the range of investments available. Alliance Trust Savings' Select ISA is an inexpensive choice for investors who want to make their own decisions, as it has no set-up charges or annual fees. Visit www.alliancetrust.co.uk or tel. 01382 201 900 for details.

Transferring stocks and shares ISAs

Not every stocks and shares ISA selection you make will turn out perfectly. And you might find the ISA you choose this year is not suitable for your needs in five years' time.

The good news is that you are entitled to transfer between funds, accounts and providers as often as you wish. But bear in mind that switching funds carries costs that will eat into the value of your investment. Some ISA providers levy an exit charge on ISA transfers, so you might be hit with a double whammy of charges – one when you leave the fund and one when you pay an initial charge to invest elsewhere.

How to buy an ISA

If you don't feel confident enough to choose an ISA fund yourself, you need to find an independent financial adviser who will make a recommendation based on a thorough analysis of your financial circumstances.

Armed with a little investment knowledge, however, you should be able to make your own selection. There are several ways to buy your chosen fund and you should consider all the options before committing your money.

It is really important to understand that, in the case of a stocks and shares ISA, you pay fees for the management of the investment. How you buy the ISA can reduce those fees. As some ISAs charge 5 per cent up front, plus ongoing annual management charges of around 1 per cent, it is worth looking into how to avoid reducing these fees, as even small charges can eat into your investment significantly over the years.

Understanding ISA fund charges

Fund managers levy several charges on your ISA investment. When you buy your ISA fund, the manager makes an initial charge, which can be as high as 5.25 per cent of the money invested. On a £7,000 ISA, that is £367.50 gone straightaway, before a penny of your investment reaches the stock market.

There is also an annual management charge to cover the running expenses of the fund, including trustees' fees, administration and investment management. Annual management charges are sometimes as high as 1.5 per cent of the value of the fund each year. This means if your ISAs are worth £20,000, then you could be paying £300 a year to the fund manager.

ISAs to buy direct

There are two types of ISA that you can consider buying directly from a fund management group.

- **Index Tracker Funds**. These charge little or nothing up front and you may be able to find a fund manager that is offering a discount on charges.
- **Investment Trusts**. These are not commonly available through discount brokers or fund supermarkets.

When not to go direct

If you know exactly which fund you want, you might think that approaching the fund manager directly would seem the logical way to get the best deal. You would be wrong! By doing this, you would pay the fees in full. The exception is at the end of the tax year – in February, March and April – when fund managers sometimes offer reductions on their ISA charges.

In the strange world of financial services, and particularly in the case of ISAs, it usually pays to include a middleman.

Discount brokers, also called execution-only brokers, are a good option for investors who don't need advice on their ISA choice. Such brokers are able to offer discounts on fund fees because they buy unit trusts and Oeics in bulk and are therefore able to negotiate good deals with fund management houses.

The discount is usually offered on the initial charge – the up-front fee that you pay when buying a stocks and shares ISA fund. This initial charge can be as high as 5.25 per cent of the investment if you buy direct from the fund manager. However, discount brokers often manage to negotiate this down to less than 1 per cent.

Fund supermarkets are similar to grocery supermarkets: they allow consumers to buy a variety of goods from different producers at one central location. In the case of ISAs, they make life a lot easier for investors as the ISA tax wrapper is held and administered by the supermarket rather than by any individual fund manager. This means you can spread your ISA allowance between funds from several fund managers. It's also much easier to switch between funds, because there's no need to move the tax wrapper itself.

Another benefit is less paperwork as you just get one regular statement from the fund supermarket, rather than individual statements from the fund managers in whose funds you are invested.

Supermarkets allow you to view your ISA portfolio online. You can choose ready-made fund packages if you're unsure about making your own choices. However, note that most fund supermarkets don't sell investment trusts, only unit trusts and Oeics.

How to choose an ISA

You can put almost anything in an ISA, from cash, bonds and shares to commercial property and gold. There are thousands of ISA funds to choose from, which is great because you're bound to find something that suits your circumstances. But it also makes your selection a bit daunting as you have to do a lot of research before you choose.

Don't just go for the funds that are being marketed everywhere in that particular year. Investors who have been seduced by fashionable funds, for example technology funds, have suffered heavy losses in the past.

Experienced investors, or those who are comfortable with extra risk, take a view on the investments that will do well in the short term based on the economic climate. Someone may, for example, think that Japan is going to do well this year and so put this year's ISA allocation into a Japanese equity fund. But this is a risky approach to investing, as the judgement may be proved wrong. Many investors who try to time the markets in this way lose money.

A more reliable strategy is to make sure you understand the principles of asset allocation. You then construct an

ISA portfolio that is spread between different asset classes, to spread risk and hopefully still meet your financial goals. For more on asset allocation turn to Chapter 14.

Contacts

Discount brokers

Allenbridge Group: www.allenbridge.co.uk

Bestinvest: www.bestinvest.co.uk

Chelsea Financial Services: www.chelseafs.co.uk

Financial Discounts Direct: www.financial-discounts.co.uk

Hargreaves Lansdown: www.hargreaveslansdown.co.uk

Torquil Clark: www.tqonline.co.uk

Fund Choice: www.isachoice.co.uk

Fund supermarkets

Interactive Investor: www.iii.co.uk

Barclays Stockbrokers: www.stockbrokers.Barclays.co.uk

Cofunds: www.cofunds.co.uk (only available through an independent financial adviser)

Fidelity FundsNetwork: www.fidelity.co.uk

FundChoice: www.isachoice.co.uk

Funds Direct: www.fundsdirect.co.uk

Hargreaves Lansdown: www.h-l.co.uk

Torquil Clark: www.tqonline.co.uk

Stockbrokers that offer self-select ISAs

Hoodless Brennan: www.hoodlessbrennan.com

The Share Centre: www.share.com

ShareCrazy: www.sharecrazy.com

Saga Share Direct: wwww.saga.co.uk

Halifax Share Dealing: www.halifax.co.uk/sharedealing

TD Waterhouse: www.tdwaterhouse.co.uk

Barclays Stockbrokers: www.stockbrokers.barclays.co.uk

Abbey Sharedealing: www.abbeysharedealing.com

Building an investment portfolio

Despite spending great effort in identifying the best investment opportunities, many investors ignore a key factor – arguably the most important – in achieving investment success. This is the need to construct a portfolio that is diversified across different investment styles, sectors and types of investments. In jargon, this is called 'asset allocation'.

Imagine your investment portfolio is a cake mixture, and you'll get a better handle on how it is put together. Some ingredients are cash, some are company shares, some are made from government bonds, and a few may even be solid gold. You need a good mixture to get the recipe right.

Research has found that asset allocation – the practice of splitting your investment portfolio among different assets such as cash, equities, bonds, property and commodities – is the key to long-term investment success. Some very clever academics in the US managed to work out that 90 per cent of investment returns can be attributed to the asset allocation mix of a portfolio. Only 10 per cent is the success or failure of the professionals who are managing your money.

Of course, there is no perfect formula for investment success – otherwise we would all be rich. But the diversification that lies at the heart of asset allocation is a simple enough equation. In simple terms, don't put your eggs in one basket, and you're less likely to lose your money.

The theory is that you can reduce the risk of your portfolio not growing in the desired way because each asset type performs in a different way to the others. Certain assets respond better or worse in different economic conditions. When equities rise, for example, bonds often fall. And when the stock market begins to fall, commercial property might start to generate stronger returns. This doesn't always work, of course, but it generally holds true.

Basic ingredients of an investment portfolio

Cash

Most investors have some money on deposit in a bank account. Great. This is the basis of your portfolio.

Cash is simple: you put your money in a bank or building society and get it back with interest on top.

Most investors need a cash cushion to pay for emergencies, such as a new washing machine, or to tide them over if they become unexpectedly unemployed. You should have between three and six months' income saved in an emergency cash fund that you can access easily. It is very important to get a decent rate of interest, particularly one that beats the current rate of inflation, otherwise the cash element of your portfolio will be losing its value. You can find the best rates for your savings at www.moneyfacts.co.uk.

Equities

Equities – another word for shares – often seem frightening to the beginner investor. The stock market seems daunting and complicated. You may own equities without realising it, for example, if you are a member of a company pension scheme. However, equities are simply a way of sharing in the growth of the economy. By buying shares you are buying a stake in a company.

If the company is a successful business, the value of your shares could rise and you might be able to sell them at a profit. If the company does badly, the value of the shares may fall.

Equities are considered to be high-risk investments, as there is a chance you might not get your money back – if the company runs into trouble, the shares may cease to have any value at all.

Equities are often used for investment growth. If you invest in the shares of a little company and it grows into a multi-million pound enterprise, then your shares will probably rise in value. However, equities can also be used to generate a regular income. They pay a share of the company profits to shareholders through regular income payments, known as dividends. Dividends can provide an income or you can reinvest them in more shares to grow your capital.

If you are investing for the long term (more than five years), experts recommend that equities should form the bulk of your investments because, although they may go up and down in value from month to month and from year to year, history has shown that they provide the best returns of all the assets over the long term. Because equities are 'volatile' (they can rise and fall in value very quickly) they don't suit short investment periods, unless you are comfortable with a very high risk strategy.

The proportion of a portfolio that goes into equities is the key factor in determining its risk profile. Very few people are truly high-risk investors. If your whole investment is in equities, you risk losing everything. For most, therefore, an all-equity portfolio is unsuitable.

It's important to spread your equity investments between large and small companies, and between UK and overseas companies. Small companies have greater potential to grow but are riskier, while big companies such as those that comprise the FTSE 100 index offer relative stability with some growth potential. If small companies do badly, your large company investments may be doing well and can thus maintain the value of your portfolio.

Most investors are far too UK-centric, perhaps concerned about committing to overseas markets. While the UK should always represent a core holding for any UK investor, it is best not to have too many eggs in one basket. A global approach to investing can offer broader diversification and greater investment potential. This diversification can lower the risk of your portfolio performing badly. An investment overseas could offset poor performance in the UK.

If you are investing overseas, you are also taking a risk with currency differences. If you are invested in, say, Japan and the yen falls against sterling, the value of your Japanese investments is worth less in sterling.

Bonds

Bonds are simply loans to companies, local authorities or the government. They usually pay a fixed rate of interest every year and aim to pay back the capital at the end of a stated period.

Corporate bonds are issued by companies to raise money to invest in their businesses. Gilts (gilt-edged stocks) are bonds issued by the government. Corporate bonds and gilts are traded on the stock market, which means their value can rise and fall. You are not guaranteed to get all your money back under all circumstances.

Bonds provide a more regular income and lower volatility (they don't go up and down in value so much as) equities. They can act as a cushion against the unpredictable ups and downs of the stock market.

Often bonds do not move in the same direction as shares. Investors who are more cautious and concerned about the safety of their investments often allocate more of their portfolio to bonds than equities.

Property

Property is fascinating to investors because it is a tangible asset: if you own a property – or part of one – you can go and see your investment. It's not a piece of paper that can lose its value overnight, but bricks and mortar that will still be there tomorrow, even if it is worth less. However, buying your own home does not make you an expert in the property market. Investing in commercial property is very different to investing in residential property.

Commercial property – which includes shops, offices and industrial premises – is a core asset to complement shares and bonds. The market can be subdivided into:

■ **retail** – e.g. shopping centres and supermarkets;

- **industrial** – e.g. warehouses and factories;
- **offices** – e.g. office blocks and business parks; and
- **leisure** – e.g. hotels and leisure parks.

Each type offers different opportunities.

You generally benefit from higher guaranteed income on commercial property compared to any income potential from residential rent. You generate this income through institutional leasing – this gives you a guaranteed, clear return for a fixed term. In addition you have 'upward only' rent reviews every three to five years. And of course, the underlying value of the property can rise and fall.

Commodities

Commodities are raw materials for production. They include agricultural products such as wheat and cattle, energy products such as oil and gasoline, and metals such as gold, silver and aluminium.

There are also 'soft' commodities – those that cannot be stored for long periods of time, including sugar, cotton, cocoa and coffee.

As an asset class, commodities can diversify a portfolio. Most assets, including equities and bonds, do not benefit from rising inflation, but commodities usually do. However, as commodities are volatile investments – their price can rise and fall very quickly – they should only form a small part of an investment portfolio. For the same reason, they are not suitable for all investors.

Asset allocation for your portfolio

When considering the correct asset allocation strategy for your own circumstances, you should look at your assets as a whole – your home, pension, ISAs, bank accounts. Most people have the largest proportion of their wealth in residential property – something that is hard to avoid if you are a homeowner. Many people also have rather too much cash in the bank – something that is easy to fix.

You need a clear idea of what level of risk is acceptable to you: can you afford to lose your money? Are you comfortable with the value of your investments going up and down over the investment period? Will you be able to sleep at night if your share portfolio falls in value?

Financial advisers offer widely differing asset allocation strategies to deal with different situations. An asset allocation model determines the amount of an investor's total portfolio placed in each class. These models are designed to reflect the investor's personal goals and risk tolerance – whether they need a lump sum in five years or 20 years, for example, or whether they are seeking income now or in ten years' time.

With a little investment knowledge it is possible to put together a basic asset allocation strategy yourself. Here are some examples.

Olivia's university fund portfolio			
Years to university	Equities	Bonds	Cash
18	80%	15%	5%

Jack's university fund portfolio			
Years to university	Equities	Bonds	Cash
10	60%	30%	10%

Emily's university fund portfolio			
Years to university	Equities	Bonds	Cash
5	40%	40%	20%

Review your investments regularly

The mistake that many investors make is to do the asset allocation work at the start of their investment career and then forget about it. But the key to successful asset allocation is to keep doing it over and over again. Make sure that your investment portfolio is suitable for your age and life stage and, in the context of children, make sure that it suits their timeframe.

Research from fund manager Fidelity found that young

adult UK investors are often too cautious and risk averse in the early phase of accumulating assets. Despite young investors historically benefiting from a portfolio that is weighted to shares, the research found that fewer than half of those aged between 18 and 34 have any of their retirement savings in the stock market.

Conversely, the research shows that older investors tend to take on excessive risk very close to their planned retirement dates. Fidelity suggest investors in their 40s and 50s should consider gradually increasing their exposure to bonds as a way to moderate risk. Particularly in the few years before retirement, you should review the asset allocation of your portfolio.

Understanding investment funds

Most people who are investing for the long term use collective investment funds. The advantage of these is that your investment is pooled with other investors' money and is used to buy exposure to a wider range of stocks and shares than you would be able to achieve on your own.

Buying units or shares in a collective investment fund instantly gives you a diversified portfolio. As you are not dependent on the success of one or two investments, this spreads your risk. A fund manager, who is responsible for picking the stocks and shares that he or she thinks will do well, professionally manages your money.

Before you invest, take some time to learn the difference between the types of collective investment vehicle – open-ended funds and closed-ended funds.

Open-ended funds

Most investors choose open-ended funds, which are more heavily advertised and marketed than investment trusts. These are the ones you will see advertised on the billboards at mainline railway stations and underground stations.

Open-ended funds get bigger as more people invest and smaller as investors withdraw their money. They fall into two types – unit trusts and open-ended investment companies.

Unit trusts

A unit trust is an investment fund shared by a large number of investors. The fund is split into segments called units, which investors buy to win a stake in the fund. The price of each unit is based on the value of the assets owned by the fund.

Like most investments, there are charges that investors have to pay to cover the expenses of managing funds. These charges can vary considerably.

There are usually two different prices:

- the offer price – the price you pay to buy units; and
- the bid price – the price you get for selling units.

The offer price is higher than the bid price in most cases. The difference is pocketed by the fund manager and is one of the ways that unit trusts managers earn money.

Oeics

An Oeic is a company whose business is managing an investment fund or funds. It is similar to a unit trust with certain key differences.

Oeics package their investments into shares rather than units. They issue shares on the London Stock Exchange and use the money raised from shareholders to invest in other companies. When demand for the shares rises, the manager simply issues more shares. Therefore, the number of shares issued can rise and fall as shares are bought and sold (similar to units in a unit trust).

Oeic shares have a single price – there is no bid–offer spread. Oeics are similar to the collective investment funds available in most EU countries. Many UK fund managers have been converting their unit trusts to Oeics in recent years. One reason for this development of Oeics is to make it easier for fund management firms to market their collective funds across Europe.

Closed-ended funds

Unlike open-ended funds, these investment funds have a set number of shares which does not change, regardless of the number of investors.

Investment trusts

Investment trusts are similar to unit trusts and Oeics in that they invest in the shares, bonds or other assets of companies and provide the opportunity for investors to spread risk. However, when you invest in an investment trust you are buying shares in a company that invests in other securities, rather than buying units in a fund.

Investment trust shares are quoted on the stock market, so you take a stake in an investment trust by buying its shares and, unlike open-ended funds, the total number of shares is fixed. However, it is important that you appreciate their higher risks and greater complexity.

Investment trusts carry a higher risk than unit trusts and Oeics because they are allowed to borrow money to invest – a process known as 'gearing'. An investment trust that is geared is a riskier investment than one that is not geared, because although the borrowings can magnify the gains, they can cause any losses to be much greater.

The value of the assets held by an investment trust might be different from the actual share price. This means a trust's shares can trade at a discount or a premium to the value of the underlying assets. This exaggerates the pattern of share price performance both upwards and downwards compared with returns from open-ended vehicles.

In the very long term, investment trust managers have the advantage of a closed-ended fund, which means they don't have to sell shares in the trust that they would rather keep when investors want to cash in their investments.

Active management versus tracker funds

The investment strategy and style of the investment is more important than its structure. For this reason, you need to get to grips with the two fundamental investment strategies: active and passive. You will be faced with a choice between actively managed funds and index trackers.

This is essentially man against the machine. Human beings control actively managed funds. Computers control index trackers. Which investment style has the qualities to win the race to riches has long been the subject of debate.

An index tracker fund avoids the whole concept of research and analysis and simply mimics a widely followed stock market index. The goal is to hold every share in an index of leading shares, such as the FTSE All-Share or FTSE 100. There is no attempt to outperform the index, or to buy more shares in any company that is considered particularly desirable or to reduce holdings in any share that performs badly. No researchers or portfolio managers are employed, as computers do much of the trading.

An active fund, on the other hand, employs researchers, risk analysts and traders. Active fund managers have the freedom to choose the companies they wish to invest in, based on their individual merit.

At an active fund manager group, investment managers and analysts around the world will look for companies in which to invest. They talk to company executives, analyse the numbers and study the competition and the market. When they have decided to invest, they keep a close eye on the company performance, meeting senior management several times a year and constantly reviewing whether to hold on to the shares.

By taking strategic views of economies, active funds might increase holdings in certain sectors to take advantage of anticipated favourable business conditions in those sectors or interest rate movements affecting a specific asset class.

Not all actively managed funds try to time the market, but many do. The turnover of many active funds is often quite high, meaning that on average their entire portfolios are sometimes traded more often than passively managed funds.

In theory, active funds are best placed to outperform in a bear market – when share prices are falling. This is mainly because an active fund can manoeuvre and adjust its footing as the investment terrain shifts beneath it. An active fund's manager can, for example, bale out of under-performing shares and replace them with better-placed stocks, or can move into cash and bonds, depending on the aims of the fund.

The charges levied by the active fund management industry have often come in for criticism. Tracker fans cite the exorbitant charges levied by active fund groups as a major reason to avoid them. If you are parting with 5 per cent of your investment up front as an initial charge to an active fund manager, this can have a huge impact on your investment's performance. However, there are ways to buy funds cheaply, through discount brokers or fund supermarkets.

There is no right or wrong answer in the active versus passive debate. Investors' preferences will depend on their objectives and the level of risk that they are prepared to accept. Putting a foot in both camps is sensible. This is often called the core and satellite approach: a tracker fund core, plus active funds to provide more specialist or higher-risk strategies as satellite portfolios.

It is important that investors in index funds understand both the index that the fund is tracking and the strategy being followed by the index manager. Most UK tracker funds have a bias towards larger companies. At present, UK funds that track the FTSE 100 are quite concentrated – dominated by financial, oil and gas stocks. If you are investing in a UK tracker, you are taking a bet on a few sectors of the stock market.

The flip side of the coin is that many actively managed funds under-perform the index that they measure themselves against. So you need to choose your active funds carefully.

If you are picking active funds at random, the chances are it will under-perform. So do your research and get a good manager. Some active managers have restrictive mandates – they can only take small bets away from the index. It is usually better for fund managers to have greater scope to turn to the part of the index that offers better potential.

Investors must ultimately decide whether they wish to try to do better than the market (and open themselves up to the possibility of doing worse) or perform at around the market level.

How trackers work

Tracker funds are a basket of equities chosen to reflect the make-up of a particular index. Thus a FTSE 100 index tracker will hold all 100 companies in the index, but this does not mean it holds 1 per cent of each stock. The funds are weighted exactly as the companies are in the index, so a typical FTSE tracker will be heavily biased towards the largest companies that currently dominate the index. On a daily basis, a computer trades all the shares in the FTSE in direct correlation to how their weightings move in the index.

Funds that track larger indices, such as the FTSE All-Share, find it is impossible to hold all the shares. There are simply not enough shares on the market at certain times. In these cases, a fund might hold, say the shares of the largest 150 companies in the index and pick the rest on a sector-weighting basis.

As a tracker fund aims to mirror an index perfectly, its performance is measured by how accurately it mirrors the index, rather than by how much it can over- or under-perform it, which is how active funds are compared.

Tracker funds often come under attack from financial experts when stock markets are in the doldrums. However, when markets recover, as history dictates they will, investors in tracker funds reap the full dividend. Trackers also tend to be much cheaper than actively managed funds.

Exchange traded funds

Until recently, if you wanted an investment that simply tracked the stock markets, you had to use an index-tracker fund. But in recent years, a new and more efficient way of tracking the markets has emerged.

Exchange traded funds (ETFs) are simple, flexible and cheap, and are becoming more and more popular among private investors. ETFs are not much different from tracker unit trusts, which are already owned by millions of UK investors. Like an index tracker fund, an ETF mirrors the movements of an entire stock market, sector or commodity, by attempting to buy shares in the same proportions as on the index they are trying to mimic. They give you the chance to buy whole indices as easily as buying a share on the London Stock Exchange.

Structurally, ETFs are a mixture of unit trusts and investment trusts. They are effectively fund-based investments that are quoted on the stock market. Because they are listed on the stock market, you have to buy them in exactly the same way as you would buy a share. This means you pay a stockbroker's dealing charges, which start from around £7, when you buy and sell. Unlike with shares, though, there is no stamp duty to pay when you buy an ETF. However, because they are open-ended, investors do not have the problem of shares trading at discounts or premiums to the value of the underlying assets.

Eligible for inclusion in ISAs but attracting no stamp duty, ETFs have the lowest annual charges of all collective investment schemes. Annual charges are generally less than 0.75 per cent and can be as low as 0.3 per cent.

Apart from lower charges, a key advantage of ETFs over index trackers is that they have 'real-time pricing'. This means that when you buy or sell, the price will reflect the value of the underlying investments at that time. Real-time pricing also means you can buy or sell quickly.

Conversely, index-tracking unit trusts are priced on a forward basis, so you won't know the price until the next fund valuation point. Normally this won't be a major concern, but it can cause problems as you can't be sure what price you will get when you sell. If disaster strikes, the price could drop dramatically before your price is set.

There are plenty of ETFs to choose from. These days you can buy into a bevy of indices based on property, overseas markets, dividends and commodities. With ETFs you can invest in major global and European sector indices, such as the FTSE 100 and the S&P 500.

Where to buy ETFs

Barclays Global Investors' iShares ETF brand (http://ukishares.com) caters for UK investors with its iFTSE 100 tracking the FTSE 100, but it also offers many other options including emerging market equity trackers, property trackers and some linked to government and corporate bonds.

Exchange traded commodities are also available from ETF Securities (www.etfsecurities.com). Other ETF providers include dbxtrackers (www.dbxtrackers.co.uk) and Lyxor (www.lyxoretf.co.uk).

How to research active funds

Actively managed funds have been around since the birth of Foreign & Colonial Investment Trust in 1868. Today, there are more than 1,600 actively managed unit trusts and Oeics alone, and then there are a wide range of investment trusts. The vast choice makes choosing an investment difficult.

The ultimate aim of all investment funds is to create wealth for the owner. Unfortunately, not all active funds cover themselves in glory. Many fail to outperform their benchmark, and there are plenty of poor fund managers out there. However, there are also some fantastic fund managers who are more than capable of providing a superior return. The question is how to find one.

The answer is that you need to research not only what the fund invests in, but also the manager's track record. Managers tend to move around a good deal, tempted by lucrative pay packages from rival management groups. Look for managers that have been in place for a while, say three years. Hopefully, they will stay with the fund for the long term.

If the manager of your money jumps ship to a rival, this may be a trigger to sell the fund. But if the replacement manager has a good track record, why not give him or her a chance.

Multi-manager funds

If you prefer to leave fund selection and monitoring to a professional, consider using a multi-manager fund. The beauty of such funds, at least in theory, is that rather than having to search the entire market yourself, you can simply buy a multi-manager fund that will find the best funds for you.

Multi-manager funds come in two types.

- **Funds of funds**, which invest in unit trusts run by other fund managers. If it is a 'fettered' fund of funds, the manager will only be able to choose from in-house vehicles. If it is 'unfettered', the manager can choose from all funds.
- **Managers of managers**, which give a selection of external managers a chunk of money to manage. There is a pre-set framework for the fund that dictates how much of the portfolio is given over to equities, fixed interest and other asset classes. The fund manager then decides which firms and managers have the best skills to run each part of the portfolio and hands out mandates telling each manager how their particular part should be run.

There are also hybrid multi-manager funds, which employ a combination of both strategies.

Multi-managers are worth considering if you want a one-stop shop – if you want to sleep well at night or only have a small pot of money, they make sense. But if you have £20,000 or more, it is better to build a bespoke portfolio.

Multi-manager funds are never star performers – many concentrate on sensible asset allocation, diversification and consistent performance. However, some fund-of-funds managers are more aggressive when it comes to asset allocation, while others rely principally on fund selection to drive their performance.

You need to be comfortable with potentially higher charges than conventional funds. On top of the ongoing charges for the underlying funds, there is a second layer of costs levied for the multi-manager's funds. But although multi-manager funds can be a little more expensive, it depends on what you are looking to achieve. Many investors find the perceived cost is outweighed by the benefits of simplifying their portfolio.

Do it yourself

There's nothing to stop you creating your own diversified fund portfolio containing a reasonable spread of assets. If you are aiming to put an investment portfolio together for your child to use to fund university in 18 years' time, perhaps include some growth and equity income funds, plus a property or natural resources fund – it's just a question of picking the right ones.

Once you've decided on your asset allocations, lists of fund recommendations are available from many brokers. Or speak to an independent financial adviser if you're not sure what's suitable.

Growth funds

The managers of 'growth funds' adopt many different investment styles, but a growth strategy generally means investing in companies and sectors that are growing faster than their peers. The benefits are usually in the form of capital gains rather than dividends.

You never get 'money for nothing' with investments, so higher-growth products are best suited to those who do not mind taking on extra risk and preferably have more than ten years before they need the money.

Smaller companies can be a good choice for growth investors as they are generally at an early stage of their development and reside in niche, under-exploited areas of the stock market that are ripe for expansion. Be warned, however, that a great number of so-called 'penny shares' also disappear without a trace.

There are plenty of UK growth funds, but the best growth often comes from a global strategy that includes, for example, Asia. Emerging markets such as Brazil, China, Russia and India are often seen as a good choice for growth investors because they are generally underdeveloped territories, poised on the brink of mass expansion. This makes them ripe for future stock market growth.

If you want to spread your risk, buy a globally diversified emerging markets vehicle, rather than a single country fund. Investing globally means that you do not have to try and pick which emerging region is best placed to mushroom.

Income funds

You could use an income fund as part of a long-term growth investment strategy, as they can also deliver great returns. If you reinvest the income you receive from the fund, you will reap the benefits of compounding. Equity income funds in particular are often recommended for investors who are looking for long-term growth.

Funds for all seasons

Not all funds focus specifically on either income-producing or growth-oriented assets. Some big global funds take a very broad-based view, with holdings in a wide cross section of companies from many different sectors and areas of the world.

Some funds simply aim for good diversification, often across several asset classes. Other types of investment, such as structured products and absolute or target return funds, aim to provide nervous investors with the security of positive returns (or at least no loss), regardless of whether the stock market is doing well or badly – albeit at the expense of the higher returns you may get elsewhere.

Structured products

Structured equity products – generally branded as 'guaranteed' or 'protected' – are designed for investors who want stock market exposure without risk to their capital, and are prepared to sacrifice an element of potential returns to that end.

Structured equity products come in various guises, but are typically closed-ended funds with a fixed term of five to seven years, promising the security of your capital plus a return linked to the performance of an index such as the FTSE 100 or the S&P 500 over that period – say 120 per cent of the growth in the FTSE 100.

Capital protection is achieved by putting most of your investment into the safe haven of cash-like investments where it will grow to the desired sum by the end of the term. The rest of your money (after costs) is used to buy equity-based derivatives. These are clever and complex products that can be structured so as to pay out the promised return according to any uplift in the index.

Bare trusts and designated accounts

Any investment fund can be used to save for children via a 'bare trust' or a 'designated account'. When you make the investment for a child, you will be asked in which of the two you want to hold it. Each option has its advantages, but there are crucial differences between the two.

Designated account

This enables you to keep control over the money you invest on behalf of a child by holding the investment in your own name but 'designating' it in the child's name. You are effectively ring-fencing the money for the child, although you will be liable for any tax due on the investment. If the income from the investment is less than £100 a year, it is treated as the child's income and is tax free if it falls within the child's personal tax allowance.

The fact that you still have control of the money makes designated accounts popular with parents. A designated account may be a suitable choice if the money will be needed before the child is 18 – for instance for school fees – or if the donor wants to retain control after the child reaches 18. However, a designated account means the money is still counted as part of your estate for inheritance tax purposes.

Bare trust

With a bare trust, the investments are still in your name but you hold them in trust on behalf of the child. Holding shares in a bare trust means that the bare trustee's name is on the share certificate as the legal owner and the child is a beneficial owner. The bare trustee may be a different person from the donor.

The money is the child's property and is treated as the child's for tax purposes. Once the child turns 18, he or she can take administrative control. To establish a bare trust you will either need to complete a simple 'declaration of trust' form or complete similar documentation provided by the plan manager that will enable you to satisfy HM Revenue & Customs that the shares are the child's. The bare trust option transfers the money irrevocably to the child specified, who cannot access it until he or she is 18.

Bare trusts tend to work better for grandparents, as this type of investment can help with inheritance tax planning. Its main advantage is that if the purchase is funded out of regular gifts from income, or if a lump sum donor survives at least seven years, it should be free from inheritance tax.

Also, so long as the donor is not a parent, Revenue & Customs should treat any dividends or capital gains as accruing to the child. The potential snag is that the child gains control of the fund at 18, and could blow the lot.

17
Funds for children

Fund managers often market specialist investments to parents and grandparents who are saving on behalf of children. Be wary of schemes marketed specifically for children, though, as they may be mediocre. Instead, focus on what's a good investment, bearing in mind that any investment fund can be used to invest for children by using the 'bare trust' or 'designated account' structure described in the previous chapter.

In general, if you want to invest in an open-ended fund, for example a unit trust, you need to have a lump sum of £1,000 or be intending to make regular investments of at least £50 a month. However, some funds marketed specifically for children can be useful for their lower investment limits – some will accept minimum investments of as little as £25 a month.

Investment trust children's savings schemes

Investment trust groups have a lot to offer if your goal is saving for a child. These can be a useful way for parents to capture the long-term potential of the stock market as they invest in a range of companies, which can spread investment risk, and many have low minimum contributions.

According to the Association of Investment Companies (AIC), a £50 per month investment in the average investment company has grown to £29,773 over the last 18 years.

Investment trusts are companies which invest in a diversified portfolio of assets. By investing in such a company, you gain access to a wider range of investments than you could normally buy yourself. This investment process, therefore, makes investment companies such as units trusts, a type of collective investment fund.

Investment trusts are similar to unit trusts and Oeics in that they invest in the shares, bonds or other assets of companies and provide the opportunity for investors to spread the risk. Your investment is also managed by an expert fund manager. For more on investment trusts, see Chapter 15.

According to the AIC, there are over 400 investment companies and these include investment trusts, venture capital trusts (VCTs) and split capital trusts, many of which have existed for more than 50 years.

Many investment trusts have their portfolios spread across a variety of company shares. The costs of investing in these are generally lower than their better marketed cousins – the unit trusts and Oeics – with management charges on nearly a third of leading trusts running at below 1 per cent a year.

All investment trust companies can be used to save for children and are available from £50 per month or a £250 lump sum. Some of them provide schemes specifically designed for children's savings. According to the AIC, many dedicated children's savings schemes have lower entry levels still, so it's worth taking the time to research the options that can really make a difference to your savings over the long term.

Investment trust children's savings schemes

The Association of Investment Companies (AIC) can provide you with details of investment trust children's savings schemes. See www.theaic.co.uk for more information. The AIC has published a list of member children's savings schemes and Child Trust Funds (CTFs), including minimum contributions and charges. For an 'Investing for children' factsheet and for details on investment company children's savings schemes, call 0800 085 8520 or again visit their website.

There are eight investment trust children's savings schemes and the providers are Aberdeen; Alliance; Baillie

Gifford; F&C, JP Morgan; Scottish Investment Trust; SVM and Witan.

These schemes often have lower minimum investments than other investment trust savings schemes. You can save as little as £25 a month, compared to £50 or £100 a month required for the other schemes. See Appendix for a table comparing these schemes.

Statistics from the AIC show that if you'd invested a lump sum of £1,000 in the average investment trust company 21 years ago on behalf of a baby, you would be able to give him or her £4,850 on their 21st birthday, while £50 per month invested over the last 21 years would have grown to £24,108. (Performance figures to 31 October 2008.)

18 Pensions for children

If you're thinking very long term for your child's future, you could start a pension scheme for him or her. Pension rules allow parents to save up to £3,600 a year in a pension on behalf of a child.

Up until 2001, when the government introduced pensions for children, the notion of discussing pensions and children in the same sentence would have sounded ridiculous. Before then, anyone investing for a child simply wanted him or her to have a decent start in adult life and would do this by opening a savings account or buying some shares.

However, due to the potentially enormous returns on a child pension, many people are taking these out for their kids to provide a far more lucrative option than anything that was previously available.

Although pensions may seem impossibly dull to a child, who thinks retirement and old age are an infinite time away, this is the most tax-efficient investment you can make on his or her behalf. The biggest difference between pensions for children and Child Trust Funds, which also earn interest tax free, is that pensions get tax relief as well.

The 20 per cent up-front income tax relief (which applies even if you are not earning) means that you don't have to invest the full £3,600 – just £2,880 (the government tops up the rest).

The magic of compound interest over long time periods – your child may have 60 years to retirement – means that even small amounts can grow into large sums. A modest £1,000 contribution at birth could net the child a very useful pension pot of £31,603 at 55, according to financial advisers Bates Investment Services. This assumes the £1,000 attracts tax relief at the basic rate and then grows by 6 per cent a year net of charges on the investment.

Typically, parents receive gifts for their newborns worth around £660, and figures from Virgin Money show that if this is boosted by the equivalent of Child Benefit (up to £75 a month) until the age of 20, children can retire with a pension fund of £618,000 at 65 – without ever making a pension payment themselves.

The downside of pensions is that parents may not like the idea of tying up their investment for so long. Under pension rules, the child won't be able to access the pension until he or she is 55. The nature of family life often involves unforeseen emergencies along the way that could call for cash and, if your money is in a pension, you won't be able to access it.

Grandparents may find the idea of setting up a pension for their grandchildren attractive, as they are in a better position to understand the benefits of saving early for retirement. However, grandparents cannot set up a stakeholder pension for a grandchild without the involvement of the child's parents, because a parent has to sign the stakeholder application form.

Because the child cannot access the money until he or she is 55, leaving a pension is the ultimate legacy. The only disadvantage is that the gift is likely to be subsumed into a larger pool of pension money and, by the time your child receives it, he or she may not even remember who made the initial donation.

You could also find that 18-year-old Jack, who wants to buy a second-hand BMW, may curse Granny and Grandad for putting £2,000 into a pension rather than into his Child Trust Fund.

The Financial Services Authority has a list of league tables that compare financial products, including pensions, mainly by cost at www.fsa.gov.uk/tables.

For general information about pensions, visit the Department for Work and Pensions' website at www. thepensionservice.gov.uk.

Friendly society savings schemes

Friendly societies have a rich history, extending back to Roman times when they were created for 'mutual purposes' such as the payment of burial expenses for members. Today's friendly societies are mutual organisations, owned by their members, which exist to provide members (or members' relatives) with benefits such as life and endowment assurance and with relief or maintenance during sickness, unemployment and retirement.

In 1992, legislation was amended to allow friendly societies to establish subsidiaries for the provision of a range of retail financial services, including the management of unit trusts, Oeics and investment trusts, health insurance and life assurance, and investment products in a tax-privileged environment.

Friendly societies are allowed to offer long-term, tax-free savings schemes or investment bonds, up to a maximum contribution limit of £25 a month, or £270 a year. The money usually goes into investment funds described as 'with profits' or 'unit-linked'.

'With profits' funds invest in a combination of shares, bonds and property. A bonus is added to your investments each year using a process called 'smoothing' – some money is held back in good years by the fund's managers so that bonuses can still be paid out in bad years. This is meant to even out the ups and downs of investment performance over time.

'Unit-linked' funds operate like a unit trust (see Chapter 15) and can rise and fall in value each year depending on investment performance.

Unlike conventional life assurance investment bonds, friendly society bonds are not subject to income tax and capital gains tax. Many friendly societies market these schemes as children's savings schemes, usually calling them 'baby bonds'. Parents can invest £270 a year for each child under 18.

Unfortunately, these products often suffer from high charges and mediocre investment performance. Friendly societies defend the high charges by claiming it is expensive to administer large numbers of low-value accounts. They say they would like to accept larger contributions, thus making their administration more economical, but legislation prevents them.

Another big downside is that the products are usually inflexible – you can't access the money easily, as policies are usually set up for ten years and there are heavy early-surrender penalties.

Critics of baby bonds believe that parents can get better returns from investments in unit trusts placed in a 'bare trust' (see Chapter 16). Advocates of baby bonds stress the tax-free nature of the benefits and the peace of mind that comes from investing in a 'managed fund' and not having to take investment decisions.

Some baby bonds can certainly be useful as part of a wider portfolio of savings, if you have the time to research them and choose a decent product. However, they shouldn't be your first choice for your child's investment.

Independent financial adviser Peter McGahan, managing director of Worldwide Financial Planning, says: 'Friendly society savings plans were sexy when politicians were, but somehow that has drooped and the old poor with-profit options available, coupled with higher charges, once again make this as appetising as used bath water.'

For further information contact the Association of Friendly Societies at www.afs.org.uk or on 0161 952 5051.

20 School fees planning

It's a personal and also an expensive choice to educate your child privately. Apart from political and emotional issues, the decision will depend on family finances and the number of children.

I've heard of one couple who started a savings pot for their child's secondary education before the child was even conceived. But few parents will be able to plan so far ahead. Most pay the majority of school fees out of available income, supplemented with loans. But if you do some planning and investment in advance – even small amounts – this will soften the financial blow.

It's very important to put your child's education in the context of the whole family's finances. If you as parents haven't started saving for retirement, then it doesn't make sense to spend vast sums of money educating a child when state education is free.

You need to make sure that you will be able to afford the full seven years in secondary school. An article in the *Financial Times* in June 2008 reported that parents who sent their kids to private school were heading to pawnbrokers to raise cash to combat the 'the astronomical rise' in tuition costs. One pawnbroker said: 'We have seen a significant increase in the number of diamond rings and other gold rings being pledged for loans.'

The number of parents who can afford private school fees is falling. In 2008, it was only people who worked in just 18 occupations who could reasonably afford to send their child to private school, compared to 30 occupations in 2003, according to Halifax research.

You really can't afford to sacrifice your own security and comfort in retirement for your child's education. Ask yourself whether it is so important to educate your child privately. Is it just a case of keeping up with the Joneses? Or do you really feel that this is the best option? Have you fully investigated the local state schools? Would it be possible to move to another area to get your child into a good state school?

If you're really set on educating your kids privately, then make sure you are fully aware of exactly what financial commitment this entails. Average annual fees can be anything from £8,000 to £11,000, depending on the area of the country in which you live. If your child wants to follow in the footsteps of Harry Potter and board, the fees will be significantly more.

The fees are only one – albeit significant – part of the outgoings. You will also have the uniform, equipment and, possibly, expensive school trips on offer that young Olivia or Jack will be very upset not to attend with all their other well-heeled young friends.

Most parents know that a private education doesn't come cheap. But the big catch with school fees is that they rise much faster than inflation. This means that if your income can just about stretch to cover young Fred's bill when he's in year seven, by the time he's doing his A-levels you'll be spending much more than you earn. So, remember to take school fees' inflation into account when estimating your total bill.

According to research by Halifax, the average annual private school fee in 2008 of £10,239 is equivalent to 33 per cent of annual average gross earnings (£31,349); in 2003 the comparable ratio was 28 per cent. It has thus become more difficult for the average earner in many occupations to send their children to private school. Among the occupations which no longer pay sufficient to fund private school without assistance from other sources are veterinary practice, engineering, teaching and computer programming.

Faced with these figures, it is no surprise that there is increased support from schools to ease affordability difficulties. The Halifax research found that schools have sought to ease these problems for many parents by increasing the number of bursaries available. Nearly a third (31 per cent) of pupils at ISC independent schools[1] receives support from the schools, worth over £300 million. In 2000, only 20 per cent of pupils received support from the school.

Annual School Fees by Region in 2007	
Region	Average Annual Fees
Scotland	£8,427
North	£7,944
Wales	£8,763
W Midlands	£9,114
E Midlands	£8,874
East Anglia	£9,396
South West	£9,513
Greater London	£10,587
South East	£10,908
Great Britain	£9,627

Source: Independent Schools Council

Finding the money

Unless you can afford to pay fees entirely out of your income or with help from relatives – often grandparents

---

[1] An ISC independent school is a private school which is associated with the Independent Schools Council, or with a schools association which itself is associated with the Independent Schools Council.

offer to help out – you will need to do one of two things to raise the funds: borrow or save.

Borrowing the money

You could borrow from friends or relatives, but this is not always the best option: money often gets in the way of maintaining good relationships. Even if they offer to lend it to you, think twice about it. However, if you're offered an interest-free loan from a friend or relative, this is obviously the cheapest way of raising the funds.

Most people go to a bank or building society for a personal loan. However, this isn't necessarily the cheapest way of raising the money. Personal loans can be expensive and inflexible – you may not be able to pay them off early without incurring a penalty fee.

A better way to borrow the money may be through remortgaging or using one of the new 'flexible' mortgages.

Remortgaging

If your house has risen in value since you bought it, or if you have paid off some of the mortgage, or if your income has risen, then your bank is likely to say yes to your request for extra funds.

Make sure that you shop around for the best rates. You may be able to save money on your original loan, plus get a better deal on the increased mortgage. There is plenty of information on the best mortgage deals available online. A good source is www.moneyfacts.co.uk. Another option is to use an independent financial adviser or independent mortgage broker to help find you a good deal, but be prepared to pay for the advice you receive, either through a fee or through commission on the mortgage you take out.

Flexible mortgages

Moving to a flexible mortgage can help you to plan your finances to pay for school fees. A truly flexible mortgage allows you to overpay, underpay, take payment holidays and borrow back overpayments. Although you may be able to draw down extra money to pay for school fees, there will be limits on how much you can borrow so that you remain on track to repay the debt.

Saving the money

Saving and investing for private education should not be seen in the context of generating one lump sum. Instead, it can be split up into separate years in which you will need individual pots of money to pay the annual fees. These savings and investments pots can be set up to mature at the start of each school year.

If you have less than five years before Jack and Grace start private school (or any particular year of their schooling for which you are planning), then don't risk putting your money in the stock market. Instead stash it in a cash deposit account, a cash ISA (see Chapter 13) or a National Savings and Investments product (see Chapter 11). You won't have as much growth potential for your money, but you'll ensure that it is being kept safe enough to pay the first term's (or subsequent terms') cheque.

Long-term investment options

Parents who have five or more years before facing school fees have plenty of investment options. The best growth potential for your money is in the stock market, but this bears the risk that you could also lose it. Stock markets have good and bad years depending on economic conditions at the time.

This means you need to plan your investments carefully to make sure that you are not cashing in equity investments to pay for a school year at a time when the markets have plummeted. If you do this, then you'll have crystallised your losses.

If you gradually move each annual pot out of equities into bonds and cash as the year approaches in which the money will be needed, you won't risk losing it in stormy stock markets as the deadline for paying the school fees bill approaches. Some investment funds are set up to have target dates for encashing the investments and go through this process for you. Fidelity's Wealthbuilder target funds are a good example of this strategy. For further information, visit www.fidelity.co.uk.

Some other more esoteric options come under the investing for children banner. These include the following.

Zero-dividend preference shares

Zero-dividend preference shares (zeros) are a share class of a split-capital investment trust and can work well if you are investing for school fees. However, they are as complicated to understand as their name sounds. You will definitely need the advice of an independent financial adviser to explain how such a product works and whether it is suitable for your circumstances.

Zeros are growth shares which pay no dividend, so you pay no income tax. When the zero matures, typically after seven years, there is only capital gains tax to pay above the CGT limit. You can stage zeros to mature when you need the money – to coincide with the start of each school year, for example – but there is no guarantee that zeros will pay out at maturity.

Traded endowment policies

These are sometimes used in school fees planning. A traded endowment policy (TEP) is a life assurance policy which the original policyholder no longer requires. Instead of surrendering it back to the insurance company, the original policyholder sells it to a market maker, in most cases for an amount greater than the surrender value.

In turn, TEPs are bought by other investors as investments offering the prospect of steady and stable growth in the future.

TEPs can be used simply to build up a large sum of capital at a specified time in the future. Their attraction lies in the fact that the basic sum assured and current accrued bonuses are guaranteed provided you maintain the policy, paying the monthly premiums to maturity.

Using a lump sum

If you receive a windfall or inheritance that you want to use for school fees, think about paying it to the school in advance as this may attract a discount.

Many independent schools have a facility, known as Composition Fees, for paying some or all of a child's fees in advance direct to the school. The amount required will vary depending on the school chosen, the number of terms required and the date of the advance payment.

Talking to an independent financial adviser who specialises in school fees planning will help here.

University challenge

A 2008 survey by the Association of Investment Companies (AIC) into attitudes towards university debt reveals that both teenagers and parents are still massively underestimating the true cost of university because they have not taken into account the dramatic impact of top-up fees.

The National Union of Students estimates that these fees will add an extra £7,000 to the debt students graduate with, so students who left university in 2008 have around £13,000 of debt while those leaving in 2009 and who have paid top-up fees will graduate with around £20,000 of debt.

Would-be students estimate their average level of debt on graduation will be £12,203, whereas parents are even further out in their estimate, believing their children will finish their studies owing just £9,681. It is important to remember the many positives of a university education, but worrying that so many parents and children underestimate the true level of graduate debt. Unless parents and students start to really get to grips with the financial implications of going to university, the shortfalls faced by tomorrow's students could put them in serious financial difficulties right at the start of their working lives.

Parental help

According to the AIC study, most parents (84 per cent) are willing to make sacrifices to support their child at university. Sacrifices might include foregoing a new car or annual holiday, or giving up dreams of moving to a larger house or early retirement. However, the sooner you start investing for your children, the better chance of greater returns. Even small investments in the stock market when your child is young can grow to large amounts by the time a child reaches university.

Research by Halifax in May 2008 reveals that over half (53 per cent) of students receive funding from their parents to help them through their studies.

Source of funding	% of students receiving
Parents	53%
Government financial support	49%
Job	48%
Borrowing	41%
Savings	36%
Other	10%
Grandparents	5%

Source: Halifax

Student loans

Make sure that you research all the student funding options before your child starts their first term at university. There is currently more than £160 million in student funding which 16–24 year olds can claim depending on personal circumstances, but often young people simply aren't aware of the support that's available.

The first place to start is the official Student Loans Company (www.slc.co.uk). This government-backed scheme offers the cheapest long-term debt available to students. Although you pay interest, the rate is linked to inflation, so in effect you will repay broadly the same amount that you borrowed in the first place. There's nothing to repay until after you graduate, and even then you only repay 9 per cent on your earnings above £15,000 – if you earn less than that you won't have to repay a thing.

A survey by Student Cashpoint (www.studentcashpoint. co.uk) found that more than 50 per cent of 16 to 24 year olds struggle to think of any types of higher education funding. The website provides comprehensive information on all sources of student funding including student loans, university scholarships, special support grants and maintenance grants. Students can also compare the amount of funding available at different universities, helping them make informed choices about where to study and how to minimise the burden of student debt.

Buying student property

Buying a property for your child to live in while he or she is at university can be a really good investment. It will help to pay your child's way through a three or four year course and then later on contribute to your retirement plans.

When your children set off for a university away from home they need a place to live, but student accommodation can be expensive and the standards can vary wildly. Buying a property in the town or city in which they are going to study can first of all ensure that your child isn't living in a hovel, but also help him or her save on rent and earn extra money by letting rooms to other students.

Student property can generate great returns because it is usually let on a per-room basis, which tends to produce a better yield than letting the property to a single occupant. However, investors must research the local area and select the right property for its particular student market. It is essential that parents looking to purchase property for their children ensure that the figures add up before they make the investment. Investors also need to make sure they are clued up about the various rules and regulations, such as those governing houses in multiple occupation (see

www.communities.gov.uk/housing/rentingandletting/
privaterenting/housesmultiple for a helpful summary) or
energy performance certificates (http://campaigns.direct.
gov.uk/epc).

Also be aware that not all university towns are a great
investment: for example, Oxford, Cambridge and London
perform less well due to high property prices, according to
August 2008 analysis of the student property market by
Paragon Mortgages. The same study reveals that Durham
delivers the best returns on student rental property.
Student property in the city – which has one of the
country's smallest student populations, with only 17,410
students – generates an average yield of 13.94%. That is
followed closely by Nottingham (13.56%), which has two
universities (Nottingham Trent and the University of
Nottingham) – and nearly 60,000 students.

Paragon's research revealed that growing – yet still
relatively unfashionable – university towns are generally
producing stronger yields than property in some more
established university locations. For example, Stoke (home
to Staffordshire University), Hull, Derby and Swansea all
perform strongly.

Bank of mum and dad

If you are a parent of a young adult – or could be before you reach retirement – you may face pressure or demands from your children to help them onto the property ladder. The Bank of Mum and Dad is one that likes to say 'yes'. So here are some ways to ease the financial pain.

Three in 10 potential first-time homebuyers anticipates financial help from their parents, according to research commissioned by the Council of Mortgage Lenders, which represents the big banks and building societies. There has always been some degree of financial help from family but it has become more common in recent years, and among younger households.

Children asking for your help with a deposit are making a challenging request, and as much as you might want to help them get on to the property ladder, you will be taking a huge chunk out of your retirement savings pot. You don't necessarily have to *give* your children the money, however: you could consider lending them the cash, either as an interest-free loan or with interest on top and you wouldn't be alone in this: a significant number of parents do expect their children to pay the money back. A survey conducted by Scottish Widows Bank found that while one in 10 graduates receiving money from their parents was expected to return the money in 1999, this figure has now risen to approximately one in five.

But how realistic is it? Can you really guarantee that you'd get the money back when you needed it? That may not coincide with when your child or children can afford to give it back. With increasing worries about retirement planning, it is completely understandable that not every parent wants to part completely with capital that they might need in future. In your 40s and 50s, it is probably time to be selfish and concentrate on funding your retirement rather than giving away money that you may one day desperately need.

If you want access to the money, you are treating it as a loan and need to decide whether to charge interest or set a deadline for when the loan is to be repaid. Some parents enter into a formal arrangement with their children while others simply trust the kids to pay it back. A formal arrangement offers peace of mind for the parent but can be less advantageous for the child. If parents are providing the deposit, the lender will lend less if the child is making interest payments.

Guarantor mortgages

An option for cash-strapped parents that gets around the obligation to give away or lend funds is to be a mortgage guarantor. This allows you to use your salary to help your children buy a property, but means you don't have to dip into savings or investments to raise the actual cash.

Guarantors are usually parents or close relatives who pledge to cover either the mortgage as a whole or any shortfall over and above what the buyer can afford to borrow. A guarantor must usually have enough spare income to cover the entire cost of the mortgage, irrespective of the applicant's own income. However, some lenders allow parents to guarantee just the proportion of the loan that cannot be covered by the borrower's earnings. The guarantee lasts until the borrower is earning enough to cover the whole loan, at which point the guarantor is released.

While this is a great way for parents to help their children get a foot on the property ladder if they can't stretch to a deposit, the main downside is that if the child fails to keep up with the payments the parents will have to step in – and that could put their own property at risk.

Where there's a guarantor available, mortgage companies will often agree to a 100 per cent mortgage, which means the purchaser does not have to find a deposit. However, some lenders only offer 75 per cent loan to value on guarantor mortgages. Most high street lenders now offer guarantor mortgages, but if you are considering being a guarantor, use the services of an independent financial adviser and seek independent legal advice as this is a complex area.

Lending to children: key facts

- Four in 10 first-time buyers receive financial help from their parents.
- Parents prefer to loan capital than give it away.
- A loan can restrict the child's ability to borrow.
- Gifting capital can have an impact on parents' retirement plans.
- Guarantor mortgages are a good alternative to gifting capital.

Ethical investing

On top of the everyday stresses of parenthood, an increasing number of new parents are concerned about how environmentally active they are when it comes to bringing up their children. Research conducted in September 2006 by Family Investments shows that almost half (42 per cent) of the parents interviewed were concerned that they should be using ethical products when bringing up their children.

If you are concerned about the impact of your investment and savings on the environment and society – as many people now are – you'll be pleased to hear that financial companies are catering for your needs. And you don't necessarily have to put principles before profits: the two can go hand in hand.

The first ethical funds were launched 20 years ago and used strict screening processes to eliminate companies that were considered 'unethical', such as tobacco. Back then, it was expected that if you had an ethical investment you would sacrifice investment performance, as you are narrowing down your choice of investments. But there is plenty of research to prove that this is now not the case:

many ethical funds do very well and can be considered good investments.

This area is now called socially responsible investing, or SRI. It encompasses investments that have a very specific stance, for example, on animal testing. It also incorporates investments in companies that may not be perfect but are aiming to improve their track record on the chosen ethical issues. Remember, though, that one person's ethics could be seen as another's eccentricities, so you'll need to do plenty of research to find an investment that fits in with your views.

Ethical funds use a variety of different strategies to select their investments. These are sometimes classified in shades of green, but does not necessarily mean these funds are environmental in their stance.

Dark green

These funds use the strictest criteria to select investments. They generally avoid companies involved in animal testing, tobacco and arms manufacture. Investment in oil, pharmaceuticals and banking is also limited. This process is known as negative screening.

Light green

These funds use a positive approach to picking stocks. They look for companies that have a good, or improving, social and environmental record. An oil company, rejected by a dark green fund, could be considered for a light green portfolio if it makes an effort to help the environment, for example, by funding research into alternative energy technology. Light green funds are generally less risky than their dark green cousins as their managers can choose from a larger range of companies.

Socially responsible vs ethical investment

Some make a distinction between 'ethical' funds that avoid companies through negative screening and socially responsible investment funds that consider all companies with the aim of encouraging change. For others, the two terms are interchangeable. Socially responsible fund managers may 'engage' companies in a discussion about their social and environmental policies.

The FTSE4Good index series was launched in 2001 to reflect the performance of UK companies that meet certain responsibility standards. There are a couple of funds that track the FTSE4Good index. For more information, visit: www.ftse.com/Indices/FTSE4Good_Index_Series/index.jsp

Ethical pensions

As pension funds own a large proportion of the shares in the UK stock market, they have great influence over many UK companies and have the power to persuade companies to improve their social and environmental records.

More than three in four UK adults think their pension fund should operate an ethical policy according to a survey conducted by EIRIS and the market research firm, NOP Solutions. By law, all employer-sponsored pension schemes have to state their policy on socially responsible investment. This includes the extent (if any) to which they take social, environmental or ethical considerations into account in the investment selection; and their policy (if they have one) directing the exercise of rights (including voting rights) attaching to investments. This does not mean that pension fund trustees have to take account of social or environmental concerns within their investment strategies, but they are obliged to state whether or not they do so.

To find out whether your pension has an ethical or socially responsible investment policy, you'll need to look at its statement of investment principles (SIP). This may be sent to you automatically or you may need to request it.

Remember that you can lobby your pension fund

trustees to adopt an ethical investment policy. Write a letter to the chairman of the trustees and encourage other employees to do the same. Also make sure you attend the annual general meeting of the pension scheme and make your views known.

Where to find advice

Not all financial advisers will have experience or expertise in ethical investment. Firms specialising in ethical investment have grown rapidly and range from large nationwide IFA groups to small independent outfits. The Ethical Investment Association publishes a list of members on its website (www.ethicalinvestment.org.uk).

IFA Promotion's website at www.unbiased .co.uk allows you to search for ethical IFAs. You can also telephone 0800 085 3250 for details.

Social and environmental issues to consider

By applying your principles to your investment strategy, you may be able to change the world but remember that there is no such thing as a perfect company. If you're looking for one, you may never find a home for your investment. At some stage you'll probably have to compromise or prioritise your principles in order of importance.

Also, be aware that everyone's opinion of what is ethical

is different. Here are some of the issues that, as an 'ethical' investor you may be concerned about.

Avoiding investment in 'sin stocks'

Many investors want to avoid investing in companies that have involvement in:

- The arms trade
- Third World debt
- Alcohol and tobacco
- Pornography and gambling
- Animal testing, intensive farming and fur

Environmental issues

Companies can respond to investors' growing concerns about damage to the environment by producing environmental policies, putting in place environmental management systems and reporting on relevant environmental issues.

Specific environmental issues that concern investors include:

- Climate change exacerbated by greenhouse gas emissions
- Use of ozone-depleting chemicals
- Use of pesticides and genetic engineering in agriculture

- Use of tropical hardwood
- Air and water pollution
- Nuclear power
- Mining and quarrying
- Use of fossil fuels

Climate change is expected to be one of the major investment themes of the next 10 years.

The Ethical Investment Research Service (www.eiris. org) is the leading global provider of independent research into the social, environmental and ethical performance of companies and provides a great deal of useful information about ethical investing on its website.

24 What to teach your kids about money

While in previous generations money used to be a taboo subject, UK parents today consider talking to children about finance to be more important than educating them about STDs, racism or religion – according to research conducted in 2008 by Engage Mutual Assurance.

With Britons' debt mountain tripling in the last decade – leading to growing uncertainty about the next generations' financial outlook – 81 per cent of parents with children under 18 say that they are making a conscious effort to talk to their children about money matters in order to prepare them for adult life.

Debt is the most common financial topic of parental education, followed by saving for the future. The only 'facts of life' to be considered more important than debts in children's at-home education were drugs and alcohol, personal hygiene, talking to strangers and 'the birds and the bees'. Money is seen as a much bigger concern than other issues such as terrorism (37 per cent), religion (38 per cent) or sexism (39 per cent).

The fact that so many parents are prioritising talking to their children about money is a reflection of the increasing strain families are finding themselves under to make ends meet. It is encouraging that so many parents aren't shying away from the topic: the needs of the modern family are changing and it's important that children are prepared for the financial pressures of adulthood.

In considering how they approach the subject of money with their children, parents should involve them as early as possible. Whilst pocket money is a good starting point, Child Trust Funds (see Chapter 12) increasingly offer an excellent vehicle for educating children about the benefits of saving little and often throughout their childhood.

Key subjects to cover

Talking to your kids about money in the right way is essential. It's not the lack of funds from the bank of Mum and Dad that frustrates today's teenagers but more the lack of decent advice from parents on how to manage money. Parents are still dishing out the age-old adages – money doesn't grow on trees, save for a rainy day and so on – which their offspring say does not help them master the financial skills necessary for modern life.

Research from NatWest found four in ten young people feel they do not know enough about money management. And while money might not buy you happiness, expertise in managing it may well do, with one in ten 11–18 year olds worried about the future and their lack of financial understanding.

Personal finance is now part of the National Curriculum but many parents back up what children learn at school with some extra help at home. Research conducted among parents and teachers in 2008 by the Association of Investment Companies (AIC) has revealed that as part of their financial education, those polled thought that their children should be learning about the following subjects, in order of importance:

1. Budget management
2. Mortgages/house buying process
3. Explanation of financial terms
4. How to obtain financial advice
5. Tax issues

Savings habits start young and die hard

Starting the savings habit young is important and clearly influences consumers' propensity to save in later life. Habits die hard, and September 2008 research from Nationwide Building Society shows that those who learnt the value of money and how to save effectively at a young age are more likely to continue to do so in adulthood.

For example, just over half (56 per cent) of consumers questioned saved as a child and, of those that did, 71 per cent save regularly now. This means that over one and a half times the number of consumers who didn't save as a child now do so regularly (45 per cent). Also, nine out of ten (92 per cent) former child savers think their savings habits helped them to appreciate the value of money, whereas seven out of ten (69 per cent) childhood non-savers admit to not appreciating the value of money now.

Pocket money

Parents have long wielded pocket money as a powerful weapon with which to influence their children's conduct. According to December 2007 research from Abbey Banking, Britain's bad boys and ghastly girls are made to pay through the pocket for misbehaving. Some two-fifths (41 per cent) of Britain's 11–15 year olds had their pocket money docked at some point during 2007, clocking up an average of three weeks worth of punishments between them, costing an average of £8.92 per week.

Pocket money is a great way of teaching your children the value of money but can also be used to explain the discipline of saving up small amounts over a long period to pay for something special.

'How much?' and 'how often?' are thorny decisions for many parents, but many plump for paying a set amount of pocket money at regular intervals, with perhaps extra amounts available to be earned by (for example) doing the dishes or washing the car. There are no set rules: 2008 research from Halifax found that the average amount of pocket money received is £6.13 per week, but research done in the same year by NatWest revealed that instead of tightening purse strings, over two thirds (63 per cent) of parents had boosted their brood's spending power, and switched from the traditional means of giving youngsters 'pocket money' (smaller amounts of money to spend as they like) towards the system of giving an increased allowance.

Of those parents taking this latter step, almost three quarters (64 per cent) cited a need to teach their children the value of money in the current economic climate. In a surprise twist, young parents are most likely to give a monthly allowance. One in ten parents in their early thirties claim to provide their children with allowances of up to £300 a month.

To cover daily living expenses, today's teens receive an additional £30 per month on top of pocket money. Yet far from being a luxury, these new allowances come with strings attached. In a bid to instil good money management, sixty-percent of parents expect their children to cover their own travel fares, with a further one in ten insisting that school uniforms are covered. One-fifth of parents expect this extra money to cover the cost of essential study items and stationery.

Tooth fairy

The Children's Mutual's 2008 Tooth Fairy Inflation Index reveals that despite the credit crunch and spiralling costs of living, the tooth fairy's generosity is ever increasing. The average cost of a child's tooth is now £1.22, up 16 per cent on 2007 which is five times higher than annual inflation figures.

Parents may think that being the tooth fairy is an expensive business – the Children's Mutual's research shows that today's lucky children could find over £24 under their pillow from all their teeth, much more than the £6.80 their parents would have received – but the tooth fairy is another opportunity to talk to your children about the value of money. Perhaps you can persuade your children to consider saving their tooth money and get into good money habits from an early age?

Kids' odd jobs economy

Crafty kids are raking in almost £700 million a year for chores and errands according to January 2008 research amongst the country's 11–18 year olds undertaken by Abbey Banking.

The research found that more than one in four kids (27 per cent) make up the odd job army. Whilst girls were more likely than boys to be making money from odd jobs (30 per cent and 24 per cent respectively), even at a young age boys are emerging as the top earners, raking in £55 per month, compared to the £38 earned by young girls.

Babysitting is the most popular way of earning extra pocket money with around half of all working under-18s earning an average £16.96 for a four-hour shift. Car washing is the second most popular means of earning a crust for an estimated 15 per cent of junior workers.

As well as giving kids a boost to their pocket money, allowing a child to take on odd jobs is a great way for parents to show their children the value of money and teach valuable financial lessons.

The top jobs are:

- Babysitting 50%
- Car washing 15%

- Washing dishes 9%
- Tidying the house 9%
- Cutting the grass 6%
- Educational Maintenance Allowance (EMA) from college 6%
- Buying and selling items at school 6%
- Walking the dog 5%
- Vacuuming the house 4%
- Paper round 3%

Passing your wealth to the next generation

Inheritance tax (IHT) may not be something that concerns you. After all, it is paid on your estate after you die. Some people view it as a 'good' tax that ensures vast wealth is not passed on down the generations, creating a social divide between those who inherit and those who do not. However, for many people inheritance tax is a great irritant, particularly if you have worked hard all your life to accumulate assets which you would like to pass to your children and grandchildren. In fact, one survey revealed that inheritance tax is now the second most-hated tax after council tax.

Inheritance tax planning is something that a lot of us don't think about until we retire. But it can be planned for long before then, if you have substantial assets or receive an inheritance. It is perhaps something to discuss with your children when they are teenagers or young adults, though it can be a sensitive subject to broach. Many children don't expect to receive an inheritance and they would rather see their parents enjoy a comfortable retirement. Others may prefer to receive any inheritance early on – as a deposit on a house, for example – rather than waiting for a lump sum when their parents die. If you opt to pass on wealth earlier, the benefit is that you can see your children and grandchildren enjoying it while you are alive.

When a person dies, they have a certain value of assets that they can leave to their heirs free of tax. In the 2009/10 tax year, this 'nil rate band' will be £325,000; in 2010/11, it's due to be £350,000. If your estate – which includes the family home – is worth more than the IHT threshold, your heirs will have to pay 40 per cent tax on the surplus, and they'll have to find that money at an already emotionally stressful time. To illustrate, in 2007/08, when the threshold was £300,000, an estate of £600,000 would have carried an IHT bill of £120,000.

Four in 10 households are at risk of paying inheritance tax, according to research by insurer Scottish Widows. This is principally because the inheritance tax-free threshold has not kept pace with rocketing house prices. Now that house prices are falling, it may be a less widespread issue for families.

It is also now possible to transfer unused nil-rate band allowances between spouses or civil partners. The amount of the nil-rate band potentially available for transfer will be based on the proportion of the nil-rate band unused when the first spouse or civil partner died. If on the first death the chargeable estate is £150,000 and the nil-rate band is

£300,000, then 50 per cent of the original nil-rate band is unused. If the nil-rate band when the surviving spouse dies is £350,000, then that would be increased by 50 per cent to £525,000.

There are, however, several ways to reduce the tax burden for your family. The first is to write a tax-efficient will. For this you will need the advice of a solicitor and independent financial adviser.

If you don't manage to write a tax-efficient will before you die, all is not lost, as your family can rewrite it on your behalf, using a 'deed of variation'. A deed of variation effectively allows the beneficiaries of a will to agree among themselves that the will should be rewritten, so that assets pass in a direction other than that set out in the will. You can also reduce inheritance tax by investing in assets that qualify for business property relief (see the HMRC website, www.hmrc.gov.uk, for information on this), as these are exempt from inheritance tax after a two-year holding period. Business property relief applies to most shares listed on the Alternative Investment Market (AIM). These are shares in small, often risky companies, but you can reduce the risk of investing in AIM by using managed AIM portfolio services.

Holdings bought under the Enterprise Investment Scheme (www.hmrc.gov.uk/eis) are also exempt from inheritance tax after two years. EIS companies must have gross assets worth no more than £7 million at the time of investment, so these are very small companies and could be very risky. However, again, you can use an EIS portfolio service to reduce the risk.

For more on AIM and EIS portfolio services, visit www.tax-shelter-report.co.uk.

You could also take out life insurance to compensate your beneficiaries for the inheritance tax they may have to pay.

KEY INHERITANCE TAX EXEMPTIONS

- **Transfers between spouses:** No inheritance tax is paid on any transfer of assets from husband to wife, or vice versa.

- **Annual gift of £3,000:** You can give away up to £3,000 worth of gifts every year to whomever you like. If you can afford to do so, you should try and use this exemption every year.

- **Gifts out of income:** Regular gifts out of surplus income, as opposed to capital, are exempt from inheritance tax. This is a little used but useful exemption. Gifts do need to be regular, and properly documented.

- **Small gifts of up to £250:** This is £250 per person, but it cannot be the same person you gave the £3,000 annual gift to. This is useful if you have plenty of cash and several grandchildren.

- **Gifts on marriage:** You can give £5,000 to your own child on their marriage, £2,500 to your grandchild and £1,000 to anyone else. This only applies to one marriage per person, unfortunately.
- **Gifts to charities:** Any gifts to charities are exempt from inheritance tax.

Potentially exempt transfers

If you give money to your children or grandchildren (or to children you care for) inheritance tax exemptions may mean that tax does not have to be paid on it. If you die within seven years of giving the money, however, there might be some inheritance tax to pay. Most gifts in excess of the exemptions above made during your lifetime are exempt at the time that they are made but are subject to your surviving for seven years after the gift is made. If you do survive the full seven years there is no liability to IHT. If you die within this period of time, IHT will be payable. It may be at a reduced rate, but this takes effect only if you have given assets away within three to seven years of your death.

Gifts and tax: time limits

Years between gift and death	% of full IHT rate chargeable
0–3	100
3–4	80
4–5	60
5–6	40
6–7	20
Over 7 years	Nil

Tax-saving actions

The most popular actions people have taken to mitigate against inheritance tax:

Making a will	62%
Setting up a discretionary will trust	32%
Visiting a financial adviser	28%
Changing ownership of the home to tenants in common	28%
Giving an annual gift up to £3,000	23%
Making a lifetime gift to friends/Relatives/charity/trust	21%

Source: 2006 research by YouGov on behalf of Scottish Widows

Useful contacts

Financial Services Authority (www.fsa.gov.uk)

The FSA is the independent watchdog set up by the Government to regulate financial services and protect consumer rights. It provides information about financial matters on its website, where you will find information and comparison tools on pension and retirement options as well as a directory of regulated advisers and companies. The FSA Consumer Helpline (0845 606 1234) can answer general queries about financial products.

Financial Ombudsman Service (www.fos.org.uk)

The FOS helps settle individual disputes between businesses providing financial services and their customers. It was set up by parliament to do this – as independent experts – and its service is free to consumers. The FOS can consider complaints about a wide range of financial matters – from insurance and mortgages to investments and credit. Contact them by phone on 0845 080 1800.

Association of British Insurers (www.abi.org.uk)

The ABI is the trade association representing the UK's insurance industry. It provides information to consumers on a wide range of insurance issues. Contact them by phone on 020 7600 3333.

The Pension Service (www.thepensionservice.gov.uk)
Part of the Department for Work and Pensions, this is a government service with information about pensions and benefits for retired people and those planning their retirement. They can be contacted by phone on 0845 6060 265.

**HM Revenue & Customs
(www.hmrc.gov.uk/ pensionschemes)**
Revenue & Customs offers Information about the tax treatment of children's savings and how to claim back tax through form R85. Call them on 0115 974 1600.

Advice
IFA Promotion (www.unbiased.co.uk)
This organisation provides personal finance information as well as a service to find an IFA in your local area. 0800 085 3250

Association of Private Client Investment Managers and Stockbrokers (www.apcims.co.uk)
This Association provides general information on share dealing. Its directory of members can help you find an

investment manager or stockbroker who will meet your needs. 020 7247 7080

The Pensions Advisory Service
(www. pensionsadvisoryservice.org.uk)

The Pensions Advisory Service is an independent non-profit organisation that provides free information, advice and guidance on the whole spectrum of pensions covering State, company, personal and stakeholder schemes. It operates a telephone helpline on 0845 601 2923: calls are charged at the local call rate.

Investment
Investment Management Association
(www. investmentuk. org)

The Investment Management Association is the UK trade body for the professional investment management industry. It has a range of guides and fact sheets for investors. Its website also has tools to help you find a fund manager or fund to suit you. Their contact number is 020 7831 0895.

Association of Investment Companies
(www.theaic. co.uk)

The Association of Investment Companies is the trade organisation for the closed-ended investment company industry. It represents a broad range of closed-ended investment companies, incorporating investment trusts, offshore closed-ended investment companies, venture capital trusts (VCTs), AIM-traded investment companies and a Euronext company. Its website provides a comprehensive guide to investment companies and a tool to search for an investment company. Contact them on 020 7282 5555.

The Association of Friendly Societies (www.afs.org.uk)
The AFS represents the friendly society movement, and has over 50 members. Between them, these organisations manage the savings and investments of over 4.5 million people, and have total funds under management of around £15 billion. Friendly societies were established to encourage self-help and personal responsibility and to enable people with limited financial resources to improve their economic status. They do not have shareholders, which means the full benefits of the products are passed onto their customers. Contact them on 0161 952 5051.

Useful personal finance websites

www.moneyfacts.co.uk
An independent and unbiased website that will help you to make informed decisions on your personal finances. Its free Best Buy charts give a unique snapshot of the best products

available in the market in areas such as savings, investments, mortgages and insurance.

www.trustnet.com

Trustnet is a free website devoted exclusively to research into investment funds and investment trusts. It has a range of educational material, plus detailed information on collective investment vehicles.

Further reading

The Financial Services Authority (FSA) has a guidebook called *The Parent's Guide to Money*, containing practical and impartial resource for expectant parents designed to answer questions about their changing financial circumstances and to help them prepare for parenthood.

The guide includes 'a countdown to becoming a parent' which sets out clearly and simply the steps people can follow to plan financially for parenthood.

The Parent's Guide to Money and details of the initiative are available to access at **www.parentsguidetomoney. fsa.gov.uk.**

The Teenager's Guide to Money is published by Quercus.

AIC Member investment company children's savings schemes* and CTFs

Any investment company can be used to save for children via a bare trust/designated account.

Management group	Name of scheme and contact details	Investment companies available through scheme	Minimum monthly contributions	Minimum lump sum contributions	Charges
Aberdeen Asset Managers	Aberdeen's Investment Plan For Children Tel. 0500 00 40 00 www.invtrusts.co.uk	Dunedin Income Growth Murray Income Trust Aberdeen Asia Income Fund Aberdeen Asian Smaller Companies Aberdeen New Dawn Aberdeen New Thai Edinburgh Dragon	£30	£150	Purchases: nil; 3% commission payable if bought through adviser Sales: £10 plus VAT per sale Annual charge: trust's fund management and operating expenses

Alliance Trust Savings	First Steps	Alliance Trust	£50	£150	Online dealing purchase or sale: £12.50
	Tel. 08000 326 323	Self Select option			Real-time telephone or postal dealing purchase or sale: £20
	www.alliancetrust.co.uk	Access to around 4,000 investments			
					Dividend reinvestment or regular dealing by direct debit: £5
					No initial charge
					No annual charge on investment dealing account

New India

MurrayInternational

Dunedin Smaller Companies

Edinburgh US Tracker

(continued)

Management group	Name of scheme and contact details	Investment companies available through scheme	Minimum monthly contributions	Minimum lump sum contributions	Charges
Baillie Gifford	The Baillie Gifford Children's Savings Plan Tel. 0800 027 0133 www.bgchildsavings.com	Monks Scottish Mortgage Scottish American Edinburgh Worldwide Pacific Horizon Baillie Gifford Japan Baillie Gifford Shin Nippon Mid Wynd International	£30	£150	No purchase charge Exit charge: £20 No annual charge
F&C Asset Management	The F&C Children's Investment Plan Tel. 0800 136 420 www.fandc.com	Access to 16 closed-end investments including generalist, specialist and alternative investments	£25	£150	Purchase: 0.2% Sales: 0.2%

Foreign & Colonial

British Assets
Trust

F&C Capital &
Income Trust

Investors Capital
Trust

Active Capital
Trust

European Assets
Trust

Foreign & Colonial
Eurotrust

F&C UK Select
Trust

F&C Managed
Portfolio Trust

Pacific Assets Trust

F&C Private Equity
Trust

(continued)

Management group	Name of scheme and contact details	Investment companies available through scheme	Minimum monthly contributions	Minimum lump sum contributions	Charges
		Graphite Enterprise Trust ISIS Property Trust 2 F&C Commercial Property Trust Available either as a Shares Account or Stakeholder Account			
	F&C Child Trust Fund 0830 136 420	Shares Account: access to 16 investment trusts covering global, UK European and Asian Equities through to specialist areas,	Shares Account: £25 Stakeholder Account: £10	Shares Account: £100 Stakeholder Account: £10	Shares Account: initial charge nil; annual charge nil Stamp duty: 0.5% on purchases; nil for sales**

	including Foreign & Colonial Investment Trust and British Assets Trust. Stakeholder Account: access to FTSE All Share Tracker Fund only			Bid/offer spread applies (covers trust's fund management and operating expenses). Stakeholder Account: initial charge nil; annual charge capped at 1.5%
JPMorgan Asset Management	The JPMorgan Share Plan Tel. 0800 20 40 20 www.jpmorganinvestmenttrusts.co.uk	The full range of trusts is available – all 20 investment trusts from the Far East and Emerging Markets sectors through to UK Growth and Global Growth sectors	£50	£500: further top-ups can start from £100	1% transaction charge (max. £50) on purchases and sales No annual management fee

(continued)

Management group	Name of scheme and contact details	Investment companies available through scheme	Minimum monthly contributions	Minimum lump sum contributions	Charges
Witan Investment Services	Jump Savings Plan or Jump CTF Tel. 0800 0828180 www.jumpsavings.com	Witan Investment Trust	£25	£100	Savings Plan Purchase: 1% (subject to minimum charge of £1.25) Sales: 1% (subject to minimum charge of £1.25) CTF No dealing fees £10 set-up fee 1% per annum annual management fee

SIT Savings Ltd	STOCKPLAN: A Flying Start Tel. 0800 42 44 22 www.sit.co.uk	The Scottish Investment Trust plc	£25	£250	No purchase charge No annual charge £11.75 (£10 plus VAT) to sell some or all of a STOCKPLAN: A Flying Start holding
			£200	
SVM Asset Management	SVM Saving Scheme for Children C800 0199 440 www.svmonline.co.uk	SVM UK Active Fund plc	£25		No initial plan management charge No annual plan management charge Sales: £30 plus VAT

Stamp duty of 0.5% also applies on all purchases of investment trusts

** With the exception of F&C Commercial Property Trust and ISIS Property Trust 2 – these are registered overseas and therefore government stamp duty does not apply

Note: Table correct at 2 December 2008

Index